170239

TEACHING
&TECHNOLOGY

THE IMPACT OF UNLIMITED
INFORMATION ACCESS ON
CLASSROOM TEACHING

Teaching and Technology:

The Impact of Unlimited Information Access on Classroom Teaching

Proceedings of a National Forum at Earlham College

With a Foreword by **Evan Ira Farber**
Director of Lilly Library
Earlham College

Funding for this forum was provided by The Pew Charitable Trusts, Lilly Endowment, International School of Information Management, OnLine Computer Library Center (OCLC), and H.W. Wilson Company.

Published for **Earlham College** by

The Pierian Press
Ann Arbor, Michigan
1991

91-228

ISBN 0-87650-293-1

The Pierian Press
Ann Arbor, Michigan
1991

TABLE OF CONTENTS

         Unlimited information access will have an impact on how teachers teach. But will more access help to make teachers more effective? Too often, teachers focus their attention on "covering the subject matter." Teachers talk; students listen. Does this motivate students to think about the underlying structures of the discipline that they're studying? The potential is great *if* teachers bridge the gap between the subject matter and what's already in student's minds—if they consider how the content they teach will be transferable to students' lives outside the classroom.

         "Informating" as well as automating the classroom isn't at all labor saving for faculty, in fact, it makes life much more challenging. However, informating holds the potential to change the way students look at learning. Teachers and their students need to move from curricular learning to planned learning; information technology provides the means by which we can influence that change. Information technology, properly applied, holds the potential to help students not only prepare for the next test but integrate experience and subject matter.

The right technology, like the best teacher, helps students take more responsibility for the learning process. Students *can* take control of what they learn and improve their rate of return on effort. Delphi, a computer managed communication program employed by Woolpy, provides the vehicle for structured student dialogue, can be used in a variety of disciplines, and can be set up for a course in 30 minutes.

The impact of access to new technology will not change the basic approach to teaching. Much of today's information landscape will not be so much supplanted by new technology as supplemented by it. More than ever, educators will have to be coordinators, helping to arrange student encounters with the resources that are available to them rather than retreating into the posture of providing *all* the information they think their students will need.

The revolution of unmanageable information is upon us. How will we respond as *teachers*? New circumstances will not require a new mind-set for literature teachers; in fact, they will make the old mind-set more imperative than ever. They will also make the old mind-set harder to maintain. Therein lies the challenge. Sudden access to unlimited materials increases the importance of making responsible judgments concerning what to read. Is it possible that the larger the amount of material available to us, the narrower our focus will become?

seems beyond our control. How do we increase our control over the infosphere? The "meme's eye view" poses the problem of filtering—of meta-filters and mega-filters. The problem with filters is there is no foolproof filter.

99   Silicon Basements and the Liberal Arts: One Dean's Perspective
Diane Balestri, Princeton University

Institutions of higher learning must help students understand how to live in a world overflowing with information. How can the ivory tower make the best use of its silicon basements? Can the "tidal wave of information" be a catalyst that will make us re-examine basic assumptions about how and what students can and *should* learn? Faculty are developing ways to use new technology in order to enable students to control a broad spectrum of information as well as delve more deeply into a discipline—to practice the skills of the discipline and to develop mastery "by doing." Will we come to see computers as the "Nautilus machines" of the mind?

109   Unlimited Information Access: "Empowering Up" Our Institutions
Len Clark, Earlham College

If the focus of education is to enable students to live lives of significance, we must empower them to do so. More than super charging, empowering involves making whole something that is incomplete. Unlimited access to information can expose students to varying theories and their critics, to patterns of data, and to the voices of others while making them increasingly conscious of the techniques they use to impose disciplinary and other frameworks on data. The challenge for teachers will be introducing students to the powers—and the limitations—of disciplines; and helping students move beyond information gathering to the development of organizational principles.

FOREWORD

THE NEW FRONTIER: HOMESTEADING IN A WILDERNESS OF INFORMATION

EVAN IRA FARBER

In recent years technological developments in information science have revolutionized the ways in which information is stored, manipulated, distributed and used. In a few years information from almost any location, using any source, and on almost any topic will be easily and quickly accessible. The concern will no longer be "How can we get enough information?" on any subject but rather "How can we sort through all that information to find what we really need?"

The effects these developments in information technology have had and will continue to have on libraries—on their administration, their finances, their personnel, indeed, on their very role in academe—have been discussed at length. Their effects on aspects of college and university administration—on the design and construction of buildings, on campus communication systems, on financial administration, for example—have also been discussed widely, both in the professional literature and at conferences. The impact of this information revolution on scholarly research and publishing has also received a good bit of attention, but what has not been discussed very much are the implications for what goes on in college classrooms, for the teaching/learning process.

Farber is Director, Lilly Library, Earlham College, Richmond, Indiana.

This omission in academic speculation is surely curious, not just because the teaching/learning process is common to all institutions of higher education, nor because what goes on in classrooms should be of paramount interest, but also because it is really that teaching/learning process which provides the *raison d'etre* for all the other aspects of higher education, even—perhaps especially—the college library. That omission struck me as I was writing a background paper for the Carnegie Foundation for the Advancement of Teaching. The paper was on the role of the library in undergraduate education, and among the many topics I discussed was, of course, the new information technology. Within ten or fifteen years, I speculated, any library would have the potential to provide unlimited, almost immediate access to practically any information in print or electronic form. That might be a slight exaggeration, I granted, but even if my time frame was wrong, or if my estimate of the amount of information that would be available was too high, still it seemed obvious that there were many, and important, implications for the role of the library and for the role of librarians. Those I discussed at length, but then—almost as an aside—I raised a number of questions about what this easy access to information will mean for the classroom teacher.

On the one hand, it will permit an entirely new kind of freedom for teaching—for providing lecture materials, for materials students can read or use for papers. But what sorts of problems will it create for the teacher? Will teachers be able to give students guidance in using these materials? After all, students will have, in a sense, the entire Library of Congress on their desktops. Will teachers have to limit the sources students can use? If not, how can they evaluate papers based on materials the teachers not only had not read but didn't even know existed? Now, when a teacher designs a course or makes up a syllabus, or devises an assignment, he or she usually has in mind a particular library the students will use; at least a teacher has a sense of the sources students can find. But with the new technology, it's wide open. Term papers may even cease to be a viable assignment because of those problems, and because plagiarism will become so easy—and undetectable. These are problems teachers never had to think about before, and will require an entirely new mind-set.

I spoke with some of my teaching colleagues at Earlham about these speculations. They suggested other possibilities and submitted more problems; indeed, they thought the issues were not only important enough for all college teachers to think about but also raised so many provocative questions that a more public discussion seemed appropriate, and so we began thinking about a conference. We found out there were all sorts of conferences on the implications of information technology for science, or for business, but not for undergraduate teaching. And there were even more seminars and meetings on computers and education, but they were primarily concerned with hardware, or software, or computer-assisted instruction. No one, it seemed, was concerned about the impact on classroom teaching of this incredible availability of information—at least, not concerned enough to discuss it in a public forum.

In June, 1987 the Lilly Endowment gave us a small grant to begin planning such a conference. Their contribution was significant: not only did it give us the wherewithal to continue, but it also confirmed our sense of the topic's interest and significance. With that assistance and encouragement we invited some outside consultants to help us decide on a format and suggest possible speakers. Then, with those plans, we began looking for major funding. Some support came from OCLC and from ABC-Clio, and in September, 1988 the Pew Charitable Trusts funded our proposal and permitted us to make the conference a reality.

The Forum on Teaching and Technology was held in Richmond, Indiana, February 26-28, 1989, with approximately 80 participants attending (a list of forum participants is provided in Appendix A). Most of them were a select group of faculty and administrators from colleges and universities across the nation—institutions known for their commitment to teaching.

The focus of the forum was on the changes in the ways people learn and the ways faculty teach, looking at how faculty from several disciplines have been and will be affected by the developing information technology. Then speakers addressed the institutional implications of the issues raised—matters of organization, resource allocation, and personnel response to change. Readers should bear in mind that the speakers were not asked to present scholarly addresses, but rather to speak from their experience and about their approaches to teaching—personal statements which would provoke discussion and encourage speculation. (A list of "Forum Issues"—suggested questions, really—that might be addressed had been sent to each invited speaker. That list is included in Appendix B.) The proceedings were taped, then transcribed and all speakers' remarks returned to them for their corrections and/or additions. This volume contains most of the material presented in the forum.

Was the forum a success? Certainly it was if one needed a demonstration of faculty concern for what goes on in the classroom. The speakers' commitment to their roles of classroom teachers is very obvious, reflecting an extraordinary thoughtfulness about their disciplines and means of teaching them effectively, and a sincere, affecting concern for their students. Certainly it was a success if the reactions of the participants can serve as a measure; they enjoyed it and thought it stimulating, and enough found it sufficiently provocative to want to continue the discussion, either at another conference, or on their own campuses. It was also successful in the many questions that were raised, some of which were addressed during the forum, but most of which simply pointed to the need for further exploration.

Why, then, do I even need ask whether or not it was a success? I suppose because we wanted everyone to come away from the forum fully comprehending the magnitude of this ongoing revolution and its impact on the teaching/learning process. We were interested, as Peter Suber said at one point in our planning, "in the effects on teaching of quick and easy access to boundless information, *not* in technology *per se*, not in CAI...or software." Or, we wanted the participants to understand the implications of what Gordon Thompson said of his English literature students and apply his concerns to their own classes: "Right now, we sometimes help students decide what 90 percent of the commentary on a work to ignore. Soon, we will have to help them decide what 99.9 percent of the available commentary to ignore." But we were not at all sure that most of the participants came away with the sense of urgency we felt.

That sense of urgency can perhaps best come from working with students in a library, helping them find information, showing them some of the newer technology, watching them trying to sort through the mass of material they collect, and then, realizing how much more material they'll get in a few years with the technology that's almost upon us. One has to comprehend the power of this new technology and, at the same time, see how students can be lost in today's wilderness of information, a wilderness that only faintly foreshadows the one the next generation of students will face. This is not a situation familiar to most faculty.

The next step, then, it seemed to us, was to get faculty familiar with this situation. That is a step we're now taking at Earlham College. The Forum, however, provided the stimulus, the intellectual rationale for that step and for raising many related questions among a substantial group of faculty and administrators. If it only did this it was a success, but we hope this publication of its proceedings will stimulate a wider audience to think about the impact of the information revolution on the teaching/learning process.

January 1991   **Evan Ira Farber**
Richmond, Indiana

How Teachers Teach, How Students Learn

Wilbert McKeachie

Each generation of college teachers is presented with a new elixir promising to cure all of our troubles, increase our energy and productivity, and make student learning painless and more comprehensive.

In 1946, we really expected student-centered, group-centered teaching to revolutionize higher education.

In the early 1950s, television enthusiasts were sure television would replace college teachers; the technological revolution would take care of all our problems. (I taught the first psychology course on television in 1950-51, so I joined the technological breakthrough.)

Somewhat later in the 1950s, Skinner described a "teaching machine" that would improve educational effectiveness manyfold (Skinner, 1958). Xerox, GE, and other big electronic and publishing companies jumped into the teaching machine business and into programmed learning. The teaching machine was going to be education's savior as well as a money maker for private enterprise.

In the late 1950s, independent study was going to save us from the great shortage of teachers expected in the 1960s.

McKeachie is Associate Director, National Center for Research to Improve Postsecondary Teaching & Learning, The University of Michigan, Ann Arbor, Michigan.

About 1960, Herb Simon wrote that computers would replace ordinary classroom teaching by 1965. That, too, turned out not to be true.

By the mid 1960s and early 1970s, experiential learning had become the big thing. I remember one father of a student complaining he couldn't understand why he was being charged tuition—his son was not even at Michigan. When I checked, it turned out that his son was getting 15 hours credit for working with a doctor on an Indian reservation in New Mexico. (We finally persuaded his father that he should pay tuition.)

More recently, we've had writing across the curriculum, and a renewed interest in computers in education.

Each of these elixirs (or fads, if you're more critical) has had some lasting positive influence, but the impact has never equalled that expected by their advocates. Thus, we no longer have great facilities for television in every classroom, and those left over from the fifties and sixties are seldom used. Revolutions have come and gone leaving casualties on the battlefield, but achieving some gains.

College Teaching Today

What has happened to college teaching? Unfortunately, little has changed since I started in 1946. Ask students, as I do on my first day of class, "What do you expect when you enter a college class?" They expect that they will listen to a lecture. Studies in which we sent observers into classrooms found that even in discussion classes with 30 students in a section, the teacher talked about 80 percent of the time. While the discussion classes were different from large lecture classes, the difference wasn't as great as we had anticipated.

When you ask faculty members to talk about their teaching, they say, "I try to cover the subject matter." In a workshop I did last year for our faculty at The University of Michigan on teaching and thinking, at the end of the workshop one of the professors commented, "I think this is really great stuff, but I have to teach accounting. I don't have time to teach thinking."

There *is* the feeling that we have to "cover the course." Parker Palmer says he gets an image of professors stretching some big tarpaulin over their discipline and trying to hide it from students. I think that sometimes it's more like "covering the corpse"—often we're burying our subject matter rather than illuminating it.

The task of the teacher usually is presenting the subject matter. The image is: teachers talk, students listen. The listening learners have the feeling that their job is to remember what the teacher says. The teacher tells them the truth—and they are supposed to get that truth in their heads (or into their notes at least) so that they can repeat it back on tests. *That's* what teaching and learning is all about.

Obviously, there are variations between fields and faculty members. I am doing research with nine faculty members—three each in biology, English, and psychology or sociology. At each of three institutions I have one representative of each of these disciplines—three at Washtenaw Community College, three at Eastern Michigan University, and three at Alma College, a private Presbyterian liberal arts college. These faculty members were nominated by their deans as being particularly interested in teaching, and volunteered to collaborate with our research team.

We have been working with these colleagues on how they go about teaching their students to learn and to think. They are all very good teachers. Yet when we ask them to look at their examinations and to classify questions in terms of three levels: (1) rote knowledge, (2) comprehension, (3) thinking, they look at their exams and discover that they are predominately at level one. So even with very good teachers, the picture of learning is one of low-level memorization of facts.

In fact, it's not very different in my own course. I lecture to a freshman class called "Learning to Learn." It's a basic cognitive psychology course intended to help students with their learning both in college and after college. On Sunday and Tuesday nights, I work till midnight or 1:00 a.m. preparing my lecture for the next day and going over my notes from previous lectures. I keep a file for each lecture, going through it for the things that might be included in the next lecture.

Most of my emphasis is on covering the content that is scheduled on my syllabus for that day. I probably spend a little more time than many faculty members in thinking about how I can get students involved; how I can break the lecture up so that I'm not just talking; how I can I get students thinking during the lecture. But for most of us, our emphasis in preparation for classes is on content, with only a little bit on teaching method. Even the thought we devote to teaching is more often on methods of explaining the content, rather than on methods of motivating students or getting students to think. We need a revolution in teaching.

Theories of Learning

How do our ideas about teaching relate to how students learn? It's quite clear that students expect the kinds of teaching that we give them. They have had lots of experience in school learning. They see their role as getting the notes on our lectures, reading the assignments (at least before a test), and somehow remembering enough so that they will be able to pass the midterm and final exam. How does the students' view of learning fit with psychological theories of learning?

When I was a graduate student, 40 years ago, the dominant theory of learning was behaviorism. Learning consisted of a stimulus hitting the eyes, ears, or other senses; this being followed by a response. That stimulus was then linked to the response by reinforcement—some kind of reward. Forgetting was believed to be a product of decay and interference from later learning. We expected that, other things being equal, probably 60 percent of what we taught in a lecture would be forgotten in a week, unless it were reviewed.

Though the emphasis upon getting students to review was good, our understanding of the role of review is now quite different. To help you understand that difference I want to give you a short course in cognitive psychology.

First, instead of learning being a process in which stimuli gets hooked to responses through some kind of telephone network in the brain, the new view is that students create knowledge rather than teachers transmitting it to them. Learning and memory are constructive processes involving what is already in the students' heads as much as what we try to put there through lectures, reading assignments, and other educational activities.

What this means for teachers is that having an understanding of what's in the students' heads is probably equally as important as knowing the subject matter. If we are to teach effectively, we have to bridge that gap between what we want to present and what's already in students' minds. As students listen to a lecture, they are interpreting it, trying to make sense out of it in terms of what they already know. Often what they already know is quite different from the blank-slate we imagine.

One of the concepts psychologists use to describe learning is called "working memory" (sometimes called "short-term memory"). It is essentially that part of the mind that is active as a student listens to my lecture. What's happening in working memory is that the student hears the words coming in but at the same time the student is making sense out of those words from things that come from his or her own mind. If I were talking in a foreign language, most students would be completely confused, because they haven't got a lot of things in their minds that enable them to make sense out of the language. Sometimes, when we are teaching a new subject matter and using the language of our field, it probably seems to our students as if they were listening to Russian or Chinese.

Let me give you an example of what I mean by limited capacity. One of the classic demonstrations in psychology is called "memory span." One memory span demonstration is to see how many numbers you can repeat back if I read you a list of numbers. George Miller at Princeton University has characterized the capacity of working memory as seven plus or minus two. He points out that a lot of the classic mental phenomena are characterized by our ability to perceive or hold in memory about seven different units, more or less.

When you get beyond this capacity, you get what David Katz, the Gestalt psychologist, calls "mental dazzle." Katz says that information is very much like light coming into the eyes. Generally we can see things better if there is more light, but beyond a certain point we get dazzled. Similarly too much information coming in overloads the working memory and we lose track of what is coming in altogether. A process called "chunking" is one of the ways we handle the limited capacity of working memory. To the degree that we can group things or organize them, we can handle seven "chunks," or seven groups of things. There is some limit on that—it might be four or five if you get pretty good-sized chunks. Another example, which shows that you can handle one chunk containing an infinite number of numbers is to put the numbers in a series: 2, 4, 6, 8, 10, 12, 14.

How can we get our students to "chunk" and to organize things? To the degree that students have familiarity with what we are doing, they are able to organize it to make sense out of our sentences. As long as I talk in a language that you understand, you can probably handle whole paragraphs of what I say as one big chunk.

That's the big difference between experts and novices in the field. Those of us teaching have structures, sometimes called "schemata," that organize large blocks of our knowledge and enable us to store and interpret information in terms of larger contexts. The novice, however, must listen word by word, just as I do when I listen to a lecture in German or some language of which I have only an elementary understanding. By the time a German reaches the end of the sentence I've forgotten the first of it, because I'm listening to it word by word. I don't have enough knowledge to "chunk" things into groups of words and thoughts.

One of the problems learners have is keeping up with the flow of information, particularly in lectures. In lectures students can't go back to clarify and re-read, as they can with reading. One of the things you have to worry about with any form of information transmission is this limited capacity of "working memory" and the difficulty encountered by people who don't have a lot of prior experience encounter.

Another problem involves "long-term memory." Its capacity is unlimited. We can remember millions of things once they are stored in long-term memory. You probably have in your memory almost everything you have ever thought about since early childhood—maybe even some things from infancy. According to some theorists they are all there in your mind. Memories don't decay very much. You can have extensive brain damage and still have a lot of memory left. Memory is apparently stored, not just in one connection of one neuron with another, but in whole groups of neurons. Activating some combinations of these results in our remembering something.

There is a lot in our minds, but the problem is that we can't get it out when we need it. If I'm introduced to someone and I see the person later, I'll probably not be able to recall the name. But I may recognize the name if I see it or hear it, which shows that it's in my memory even though I couldn't recall it. One of the big problems students have is retrieval—they get things into their heads but can't get them out.

Psychologists have learned a good deal more about the kinds of things that cause forgetting. The problem is usually not so much in the retrieval process as in the way the information has gotten into people's heads in the first place.

In general, to the degree that we've learned something very specifically, in a specific place, within a specific context, we can remember it in that same place and same context. Give a test question using the same words as the textbook and students will remember it. Education, however, has to do with remembering things in new situations, using knowledge at a different time and in a new context, transferring skills to new situations. If you learn something just by rote memorization, it's very difficult to retrieve it in a new situation where you want to use it later. Retrieval generally is going to be much easier if you have learned something in different ways and different contexts. We call this "encoding variability."

A couple of words have been used by different theoreticians to describe this process for promoting better learning. One word is "elaboration," which carries with it the notion of learning actively, relating what is being learned to past learning, putting it into one's own words—explaining, questioning, summarizing.

The other term dealing with the same phenomenon is "deep processing." The more you think about something—the more you've processed it in a deep, thoughtful, mindful way—the more likely that you will be able to retrieve it later. For example, when one studies a chapter in a textbook, deep processing involves trying to see what the author is trying to get across, how this chapter relates to what the author did in the previous chapter, and how it relates to what else you know.

Teaching

What does this have to do with teaching in a modern context? It has a good deal to do, I believe, with thinking about the impact of technology on teaching. It suggests—if I'm correct—that education has to do with what is transferred to new times and new situations rather than with pouring knowledge into empty heads. It means that we've got to worry more about the contextual nature of knowledge—about how the content we teach will be transferrable to students' lives outside the classroom.

It probably also means that we need to try to be more explicit about why we are doing what we are doing and about the structures of our disciplines. I said that the mind has unlimited capacity. The recent movie, "Rainman," is about a person who had a tremendous memory for dates, numbers, and the like, but very little ability to function in the real world. The head of neuropsychology at Utah who studied the real person on whom the movie is based said that this person has a photographic mind. He remembers everything. Photographic memory is not a common thing, but many children have photographic memories up to age 10 or 12. Why does it disappear? Probably because photographic memory is not very useful in the real world. If you remember everything that's happened to you, how do you use it in new situations? To use our past knowledge we have developed words and concepts that enable us to summarize large chunks of experience and to relate them one to another. Thus, teachers are not just transmitting knowledge *per se*, but are transmitting concepts or structures of knowledge that enable students to fit new information into schemata (structures) that can be used in varied and flexible ways.

In addition to thinking less about covering all the facts and more about teaching conceptual structures, we need to think about how our students learn the material. When we make assignments, we need to be explicit about why we are making the assignment and why it's important for students to do it—write a paper, read a textbook, work on a team project, or whatever learning methods are assigned.

Frequently we aren't even very clear in our own minds about why we ask students to do the things we assign. In our research, we have found that when we started talking to the faculty members about why they were doing this or that, they really hadn't thought about it—it was just the way it had always been done. Our collaborating faculty members say that it has been useful for them to think about the purposes and theory of instruction they implicitly had in mind. I hypothesize that it is not only useful for us to have some notion as to why we require students to do certain things, but it also will be useful to our students in developing more useful theories of their own learning if they see why, for example, it's important to compose an essay rather than to copy it out of the *Encyclopedia Britannica*. Writing essays involves elaboration; it involves practice in thinking.

Psychologists conceive of intelligence, not so much as something that's built-in at birth, but as a set of learnable skills.

Essentially what we are doing, as we teach students how to learn and how to think, is building their intelligence. We know intelligence grows during college. We don't know very much about how it grows, but presumably it has something to do both with the accumulation of knowledge and with the development of general skills of thinking and learning that are useful throughout life.

Motivation

What are other implications of this theory? Our own research at NCRIPTAL suggests that we have to go beyond cognition to another set of variables. Our research group has developed a questionnaire called the "Motivated Strategies for Learning Questionnaire" that deals with students' motivation for learning as well as the study skills they use.

My colleague, Paul Pintrich, identified five groups of students. "A" students tend to be highly motivated and to have good strategies for learning. Students with poor grades tend to have poor strategies for learning and are also low in motivation. Often they feel that they would fail even if they tried to achieve.

But there are three other groups who are somewhat different. One group has good learning strategies—that is, the students know how to elaborate, to "deep process"—but they have relatively little interest in the course and thus they are not using the abilities they have. Another group has good learning strategies, values the course, and would like to do well, but the students have a very low sense of self-efficacy. They feel they are not very good students, and they don't do particularly well. The third group consists of students who are interested in the course, have high motivation but poor learning strategies, and are high in anxiety. They fear tests, and generally lack self-confidence. All three of these groups get grades around the average.

I suggest that effective teaching not only gets students to think about the underlying structures of our fields but also develops motivation. The three kinds of average students I talked about illustrate two elements of motivation. One element is developing an interest and a sense of value of learning what we are teaching. The other element, which we sometimes forget, is giving students some sense that they *can* learn this subject matter. One of the big problems in math and science instruction is that some students come in with a sense that "this is not my bag; it's not something that I'm good at."

In a sense, students are rational in their investment of effort. If you think that there is very little probability of attaining something that you want very much, you are not very likely to invest a lot of work in it. Thus, students who lack a sense that there is a real probability of success are not going to work hard. Such students need a lot of encouragement and experiences of meaningful achievement.

Technology

What's the impact of technology? I can't make predictions, but I can ask some questions.

One of the problems of unlimited information is the problem of access, and that goes directly to the question of conceptual structures. How do you develop structures in the computer or the data source that match the structures in the students' minds so that they can use some kind of organized framework to get the information that they need—and not be overloaded with 100,000 references that they can't possibly handle? Finding out what students think about the world is important.

One of the big areas of research in cognitive psychology is the area of computer-human interface. How do you match the hardware and software with the way people think and approach computers? That will be the key issue determining whether it's 10 years or 15 years or 50 years before we achieve the potential usefulness of computers.

We need to think also about differences between disciplines. George Leith, dean of the College of Cape Breton in Nova Scotia, suggests that there are three kinds of structures in college courses. One is a hierarchical or linear structure in which one thing builds on another. Math and science probably best represent that.

Leith suggests that a second set of disciplines have a network structure in which one thing doesn't necessary follow from another, but things are connected like a big fish net with nodes and connections between the nodes. You can start on any node and get to other places in the network. It's not necessary that you start at the beginning and build in a linear or hierarchical fashion.

Leith suggests that other disciplines are in between these two structures. He likens this structure to a spiral or a helix. You can start in a number of different places, but after you've gotten a number of basic concepts, you can move up to a higher level, develop some more concepts, and then move to a higher level still. It's not strictly hierarchical, but there is some kind of upward progression.

Jan Donald, head of the Centre for Teaching and Learning at McGill University, has found something like this in interviewing faculty about concepts in their field. She finds that in the sciences, when you ask professors to describe key concepts, they come out with a relatively limited number that they expect the students to know. In the social sciences, key concepts grow to the hundreds. In the humanities, it's much more difficult to identify the core. Our research group has developed a measure called the "ordered tree," in which we ask faculty members to give us some key concepts and then to describe the relationship between these concepts (Naveh-Benjamin, McKeachie, Lin, & Tucker, 1986). That task is relatively easy for our biology teachers to do and fairly easy for the psychology teachers to do. It's difficult for the English teachers to do.

Our experience in interviewing English teachers is that they do come up with things that fit into our ordered tree, but that their concepts are more procedural—involving ways of approaching things. How do you build on a concept such as "irony?" It's not a concept that links easily to others in the same hierarchical way that my general concept of memory might be linked to subordinate concepts of working memory and long-term memory. Educational technology needs to look at these differences between disciplines, both in the way the subject matter is organized and in the way the students think about them.

One of the most important educational developments in the last few years has been the increasing use of peer learning techniques, which turn out to be remarkably effective. Ten or 15 years ago, the National Science Foundation decided to support some experiments in Utah linking computers with videodisks (this was when videodisks first came out). The project was run by one of the best educational psychologists in the business, Vic Bunderson. The researchers were working with a biology professor putting units of biology on the videodisks, linking the material to material on computers and print. The researchers then compared student learning with the "intelligent-video-discs" to learning of students in regular biology classes. The programs were revised to become better and better. Students could interact with the computer and ask questions, could call up pictures of plants bursting into flowers, and more, and could get references as well as verbal and visual material. The developers eventually got the intelligent videodisks to be as effective as the professor's own lectures on the same unit. With additional development the computer-videodisk units were as effective as discussion sections. That still was not good enough, and they kept working on improvements. But during the time I was on the NSF evaluation team they never were quite able to do as well as if the students met and talked among themselves about the same material based upon their studying of the textbook. Peer learning was dramatically superior. Generally other research also shows that peer learning is very effective.

Jane Schubert at the American Institute of Research has studied the impact of computers on elementary and junior high school girls' learning. Many families in the area she studied have home computers. She found that the program enhanced the girls' relationships with their fathers, because fathers are typically the computer buffs in the family and so interacted with daughters more than they had previously.

Several studies have also suggested that students learn more if they're working in pairs on computer terminals rather than as individuals. Schubert studied the effectiveness of computer learning with same sex pairs, different sex pairs, and single students at a computer. In general, she found that pairing worked better than singles, but certain combinations didn't work. For example, when a boy was paired with a girl, the boy sometimes assumed that the girl wouldn't understand. When they ran into a problem, instead of working it out together, the boy would just do the problem and not explain it or share the problem-solving process. That's one of the problems in peer groups—if the members don't actually "elaborate" by discussing and thinking about it together, you are not going to get the advantages of peer learning.

Essentially my message is that the effectiveness of technology in education will depend upon what goes on in students' heads. If computers encourage more thought, they will be a great asset; if the student-computer interaction is mindless, the potential will be lost.

REFERENCES

Naveh-Benjamin, M., W.J. McKeachie, Y.G. Lin, and D.G. Tucker. "Inferring Students Cognitive Structures and Their Development Using the Ordered Tree Technique." *Journal of Educational Psychology* 78:2 (1986): 130-40.

Skinner, B.F. "Teaching Machines." *Science* 128 (1958): 969-77.

HOW TEACHERS TEACH, HOW STUDENTS LEARN: CREATING INTELLECTUAL TRAMPOLINES

FRED GOODMAN

Here are seven names that should be easy to remember based on what Wilbert McKeachie has said. (If you remember each name and why I included it, I'm doing well): Shoshana Zuboff, Jacob Bronowski, Ivan Illich, Norbert Wiener, Suzanne Langer, Frithjof Bergmann and Mohamar Kadafi.

In the age of the smart machine Shoshana Zuboff suggests that we need a word, something other than "automate," to describe this round of technological revolution. We not only "automate," we "informate" this time around. We inform the person who is using the machine tool, information is added as a result of employing technology. But here I should do a little bit of myth-bashing. The myth is that technology is a laborsaving device. Not in education. It is not a laborsaving device. There is nothing we are talking about here that's a laborsaving device.

Your work is going to be much, much harder as a result of the technology that surrounds you. I use the notion of informating with respect to the CONFER computer conferences that I require of my students. I am a voyeur in terms of what they are saying about my lectures. I know from my work in technology that it's very easy to imagine the technology that extends and amplifies the work of my mouth. I know it's very hard to use technology to enhance my ears—it's very hard for me to extend the number of conversations

---

Goodman is Professor of Education, The University of Michigan, Ann Arbor, Michigan.

I can hear. Technology is not very good at that. Compressed speech doesn't do you much good—you may speed things up by, maybe, a factor of three or four. However, there may be another way to employ technology to this end. If I can go into each lecture knowing much more about the way I was interpreted in the prior lecture—by reading what students say in CONFER about that lecture, by "eavesdropping" on their discussion—that's a great advantage.

It's here that I want to bring in the name of Jacob Bronowski. Bronowski talks about scientists telling the truth in the sense that they say what they mean—not in the sense that they speak with a "pipeline-to-God" kind of truth.

Is to say what you mean the same as to mean what you say? My students, since I use a lot of metaphors in class, will get on CONFER and say, "Why doesn't he say what he means? Why does he use a metaphor?" So I "get on CONFER" and explain that I would say what I meant directly and literally if I could say it that way. I explain that I'm using a metaphor in order to get a very complex point across. I want to model that for my students. I want to help break down the image that somehow lecturers tell the truth in the sense of describing reality as it really "is," and switch it around to the image that lecturers say what they mean to the best of their ability. That's often not good enough for the students, but it will have to do. Ultimately, most professors, I think, do mean what they say; it's just so much harder to say what you mean without going on for hours and hours.

Don't you believe, sincerely, that Bill McKeachie means what he says? It's unthinkable that he does not. He may not be able to say exactly what he means, but he means what he says. By the way, if business people and politicians were to follow Bronowski's lead on this point, wouldn't it be nice? What would happen if all business people and all politicians could be expected to mean what they say all the time. That might be an absolutely revolutionary lesson to be learned from what scientists do.

The third name in getting to the heart of what I want to say is Ivan Illich. Illich once described learning as either incidental, curricular, or planned. Most of us learn what we learned incidentally. My son called the white stuff that came out of the carton "more" for a long time. He'd hold up his cup and say "more" and we'd pour the white stuff out of the carton. We'd then see his cup a little empty and we'd get the carton and ask if he wanted "more," and in it would go. I don't ever remember waking up in the morning and going down and saying to my wife, "Let's teach him 'orange juice' this morning." He simply learned his language incidentally.

As for curricular learning, it has something to do with the little carriages that ran around the track in the Roman coliseum. I take it a curricle was the carriage; the curriculum was the race course. That's my best definition of curriculum—just running around the track going in circles. That's the way it feels to the students in many cases, I suspect. Illich says curricular learning is learning to play the role of student.

Then there is planned learning, which can take place even in the context of curricular learning. Here's where technology comes in. I pretty well decided as a professor of education that the only way I can survive at The University of Michigan is to take the attitude, "If you can't lick 'em, join 'em." I think that's where we are going to go with respect to technology. I am an absolute unabashed technologist, because I think that I can do an awful lot to change curricular learning into planned learning and let lecturers do what they do best—stand up in front of classes and try to mean what they say and say what they mean to the best of their ability.

The way I attempt to achieve my objectives is very simple. I have a blue notebook here that was produced by the students of Political Science 353: The Arab-Israeli Conflict. It, and ones like it on other subjects, are distributed to over 1,000 secondary school students in 13 countries. What's going on here? The university students are preparing this material so they can perform well in a simulation game of the Arab-Israeli crisis, played over CONFER. But, for $250 we will sell high schools a country in the Middle East. The high school students open up this notebook to, say, the page where they find, "You are King Faud. You, King Faud, were born in the 1920s, the sixth son of blah, blah, blah." This was written by an undergraduate student in Political Science 353 with the benefit of a very sophisticated lecturer and excellent undergraduate library reserve service. They had already put together the documents that the students need to produce a good profile of King Faud. The undergraduates probably can enhance their work by doing online searches, and the like, but the Reserve Desk helps them get started. We make students in that undergraduate Political Science 353 class responsible not only for their own learning, but for producing this book so that younger students can play the roles accurately. They're responsible for providing that documentation to thousands of high school kids, and they better get it right. They use their word processors, send the profiles in to the mainframe computer, and we edit them over the summer. Then it goes out.

I'm talking about using telecommunications in order to break down the cloistering effect of the classroom. The students are expected to learn how to participate in peer group learning—all that sort of thing—and not to let the group down as they participate in a simulation game themselves. At the same time they are going to impact people out there in the high schools, and do so in the very near future. As a result, they look at their lectures less as a matter of getting ready for a test, less as a curricular learning experience, and more in terms of how they can come to class and use that class to plan their learning and be responsible for what they have learned. I'm speaking now about getting equity into our discussion. It really needs to be there. If a student can imagine that he or she is using technology in a way that improves access to the world's literature, not just for himself or herself but for a whole bunch of people that may never come to The University of Michigan, we are changing the whole view of why students are there. No longer are they there selfishly just to learn for themselves...although they better do a good job of that too or their classmates playing the game will let them know about it. It's a very complicated point to make.

In another simulation exercise we disinter 67 people and add 3 living ones and they "go to Philadelphia" to rewrite the Constitution. We also are providing an environmental impact statement to the world bank for a dam in Zaire. In that one Ghandi is talking to Lee Iacocca about the consequences of such an enterprise.

Nobody playing those games knows who the other characters actually are till after the game is over. You don't know whether King Faud is white, black, male, female, old, or young. When the game is over you say, who are you really?

We are stirring the pot. I think that I'm not going to try to change the way instruction goes on at The University of Michigan by automating *the classroom*. I'm going to let the classroom work pretty much the way it works and then change the way the students look at that learning—try to switch it from curricular learning into planned learning, in the very same sense that a Spanish class switches from curricular learning to planned learning if you are going to Spain at the end of the term.

Next: Norbert Wiener. He made a wonderful, wonderful contribution to the subject of artificial intelligence. He said, "If you are going to use a machine as an analog to the brain, don't forget that you must never unplug the machine, you must never erase the disk completely, you must always write every program on top of the original program that's on that disk, because we can't count on erasing any part of our long-term memory perfectly."

Can you imagine writing a computer program on top of a disk that had never been erased, always trying to fix the first one rather than starting over with a fresh disk? That's the way artificial intelligence should be looked at. Just don't take advantage of the complete erasability *of the computer's complete erasability* if you want to think about it as an analog to the human being.

Suzanne Langer is on this list because I saw her quoted in Stewart Brand's book on the creation of an artificial intelligence lab at MIT. She reminds us that visual images are not discursive in the same way that language is, and if you are going to describe something in prose you indeed have to remember the whole sentence, the whole paragraph in order to digest the whole thing. In teaching math with the NeXT computer, for example, you can teach with three-dimensional animated pictures and the mind's eye will articulate things very differently.

Something new under the sun is possible here and Langer was one of the earlier ones to point it out. I like to tease Lou Kleinsmith, a biologist and one of the finest teachers I've ever seen, that when he employs the teaching programs he designed (incidentally with the help of his fifth-grade daughter) on a Commodore computer that he isn't doing anything he couldn't do at the blackboard with colored chalk and 100 hands. That's Suzanne Langer's point. In Kleinsmith's programs you can see things moving around and coming together in ways that you just can't see if you are talking about them linearly or reading about them linearly. We are not even looking in the right place unless we are looking at the visual graphics automation aspect of this technology. It goes well beyond word processing.

Frithjof Bergmann, the philosopher at Michigan, is on my list because he says in order to teach anything, we probably have to teach less. Don't think of the teacher as a juggler. Think of the students as jugglers and the teacher as the juggler's assistant. A student is trying to juggle six plates and the teacher has got to come up and watch that juggler's style and at just the right time, slip the seventh plate in. With a whole class full of students, teachers are going to run around saying, "Here's a plate, here's a plate, here's a plate." Then the teacher is going to give them an exam and say, "Are you holding the seventh plate?" All the rest of the crockery is on the floor. They're holding the seventh plate and the teacher gives them an "A." **NO**. The teacher must recognize that those people are constructing knowledge, and the teacher's task is to help them construct the knowledge that they are actively juggling.

Ray Tanter, the lecturer in Political Science 353, is probably famous for many things (an interesting one, as I understand it, is that he was once on the National Security Council and Oliver North took his place). Ray is outstanding at being the jugglers' assistant, because people come to him and say, "What am I going to do about this, what am I going to do about that," because they are playing complex political science games over CONFER during the entire term and trying to be informed by him at just the times they need help.

That leads me to Mohamar Kadafi. An undergraduate was coming out of a colleague's house after a face-to-face debriefing on the Arab-Israeli conflict simulation. It was December, it was cold, I was over there carrying my microcomputer out because we had done a little electronic scoring system for showing the students in color graphics how they had done. As I started down the stairs, this fellow who had been role playing Mohamar Kadafi was coming out the door with a friend of his and he stopped and he said, "I don't want to close this door." I pretended that I dropped something so I could eavesdrop a little and he said, "I don't want to close Edgar's front door."

His buddy said, "Why's that?"

He said, "When I close this door it marks the end of the first time in four years that I felt important at The University of Michigan."

We had greatly enhanced his ability to feel important by providing him with the technological matrix that allows him to play this game from any computer console anywhere on campus. I don't think we are looking in the right place if we simply try to automate the classroom as we know it. I think we should be automating environments, creating intellectual trampolines—Thomas Kuhn might call them disciplinary matrices—so we can get students up and teach them to do tricks on them.

Let's support and enhance instruction as we know it by surrounding it with all the opportunities I'm suggesting. Otherwise we are going to be sitting around bemoaning the fact that there is still a vast majority of us who don't know how to use the overhead projector.

HOW TEACHERS TEACH, HOW STUDENTS LEARN: THE MYTH OF TECHNOLOGICAL DETERMINISM

CHARLES HUFF

My purpose today is to suggest what does and does not—and what should and should not—determine the uses of computing in higher education. More succinctly, I intend to debunk technological determinism. But I also hope to suggest several alternative determinants of the use of computers in education. These suggestions will make both the technophiles and the technophobes dislike me—an indication that I may be on the right track.

Technological determinism is the idea that the technology drives us rather than us driving the technology. The strong view of technological determinism is as follows: if a technology can be developed, it will be developed, it will be put to the use that the developers intended, and it will have the effect that the developers intended. Politely put, this is bunk.

The view of people who hold this persuasion is that more technology always is better—more in terms of more hardware, faster hardware, more software, more complex software. "Better" is often measured in terms of millions of instructions per second (MIPS), random access memory (RAM), read only memory (ROM), bits per second (BAUD—after the Frenchman Baudot). It is easy to be seduced by these quantities; they are easy to measure—unlike the stuff educators usually deal with (knowledge, understanding, insight,

---

Huff is Assistant Professor of Psychology, St. Olaf College, Northfield, Minnesota.

skill, wisdom, etc.). Schools can use these easily measurable things to symbolize their commitment to forward thinking and innovation in education (Schonfield & Verban, 1988). And it is the myth of technological determinism that supports this symbolic use of computers. So, let's examine this myth.

The social effects of computing are notoriously difficult to predict, and this leads me to think that technological determinism must be wrong. For example, in 1879 the chief engineer of the British Post Office, Sir William Crease, testified to the House of Commons about a new invention—the telephone.

> I fancy the descriptions we get of its use in America are a little exaggerated. Few have worked at the telephone much more than I have. I have one in my office, but more for show. If I want to send a message, I use a sounder or employ a boy to take it.

Partly as a result of this fellow's testimony, the British post office did not buy the patent to Alexander Graham Bell's invention. Sir Crease expected little benefit from the telephone; Mr. Bell expected more and was shown to be correct.

Inventors and innovators are not always so successful in their predictions, though. Here is a quote from Thomas Edison in 1922:

> I believe that the motion picture is destined to revolutionize our educational system and that in a few years it will supplant largely, if not entirely, the use of textbooks.
>
> I should say that on the average we get about two percent efficiency out of school books as they are written today. The education of the future, as I see it, will be conducted through the medium of the motion picture...where it should be possible to obtain one hundred percent efficiency.

The motion picture, even though it was a success commercially, was a failure in terms of Edison's glowing predictions. And though Bell's telephone took off, many refinements on it were flops: Bell never could get much interest in his "triple mouthpiece" for simultaneous speakers, and AT&T has introduced the "picture-phone" repeatedly since 1929 with little response (you can buy one now, but I expect you won't).

The simple fact is that most innovations fail (Rogers, 1983). And those innovations that do succeed generally have very small social impact. Even if a technology succeeds (like the overhead projector) it is often used in a traditional manner and does little to change society (in our case, education). Those of us who are trying to predict the future of technology and education need to tell the difference between things like the overhead projector, which has had very little social impact, and the telephone, which has had a great deal of social impact. This is a an extremely difficult problem and I promise I'm not going to solve it for you.

But here are some hints from the research: The computer has, so far, had educational effects more along the line of the overhead projector (Cuban, 1986). Rich, white, upperclass schools get them, and use them for traditional purposes—like drill and practice or word processing (Becker & Sterling, 1987). Computers may radically change the way we educate ourselves, and I will have at least one suggestion about how this might work. But the evidence so far is not compelling. Faculty will not adopt a technology "because it is there."

Now that we have laid to rest the claims of technological determinism (and left open the question of the success of computers in college education), let me give you some hints about what some of the important determinants of computing in education are. In making these observations, I am generalizing from the past 20 years of social science research about the use of technology in organizations, colleges being just one kind of organization.

In terms of the impact of any technology in an organization, the politics, culture, and mores of the organization are at least as important as the technology itself in determining the effects of the technology (Kraut, Koch, & Dumais, in press). Secretaries can be trained to do a wide variety of tasks on computers or they can be "ghetto-ized" in word processing pools. A police officer's life can be made easier with mobile access to computerized databases, but that same access can be used to track her performance. The difference between these approaches has nothing to do with the technology, it has to do with how an organization uses a technology.

For example, we've looked at undergraduates as they come into Carnegie Mellon University and experience the culture shock of college—and, in addition, a highly computerized college. They have complained to us about sitting in sterile computer labs with whitewashed walls. They feel the institutional choice that Carnegie Mellon made in setting up the labs this way alienates them. You sit in front of a computer and there are dividers between you and other people—you can't talk to anyone else. There are no lounges close around to allow you to communicate with other people easily. Many of the complaints students voiced had to do, not with the computers themselves, but with the way they were made available, or with the "help" they got from local hackers. For these students, it was not the technology that alienated them, it was the architecture. The same computers and software would have been fine if arranged differently in more humane surroundings, and with help from people who could speak English rather than "hacker-ese." By the way, Carnegie Mellon has responded admirably to these complaints and has changed the structure of many of its computer labs.

Another member of our research group at Carnegie Mellon (Weisband, 1986) studied the organizational barriers to faculty trying to develop software. She found that one of the reasons it's difficult to get faculty—at least tenured faculty—to develop software is that organizational rewards are generally given for contact hours with students or for doing one's research, not for activities such as developing software. It is too large a risk for untenured faculty to develop software. This is a problem the organization can address and, again, is not a problem with the technology itself.

Thus, organizational factors explain a lot of the effects of the technology. And the organizational factors are (to some extent) more in our control than is the technology. We can plan those effects or we can leave them unplanned. We can, without thinking, put the computers up against the wall with little dividers between people. We can, without considering the effects, make computers available only to those who can pay for them. I hope we won't. We should be active in determining the impact of technology instead of letting someone who developed the hardware, or who developed the software, or who made the lab tables make our decisions for us.

I promised to discuss how I thought computers might revolutionize education. And here is where my remarks are really a reply to Bill McKeachie. I am struck by his data that the most effective way of improving teaching in colleges today is by "peer learning"—students teaching each other. This is a place where computers can, and have been shown to, contribute.

One of the facts affirmed by past research is that computers don't alienate people, they connect them. When computers first began to filter into schools, many people were afraid that we would produce a bunch of little hackers with their eyes lying out on their cheeks staring at computer screens (Weizenbaum, 1976). This has not happened. In fact, if you look at the research, or if you go into an elementary school now, what you find is that children sit together around the computer talking—or they use the computer to talk to each other. The computer has become a social object. One of the most comprehensive studies of the "hacker syndrome" available indicates that computers don't isolate these people (Shotton, 1989).

This is also true at colleges, I expect. There is a great deal of talking, some of it quite heated, around the terminal. These students derive a lot of their knowledge by interacting with their peers. And teachers at Carnegie Mellon, St. Olaf, and a host of other institutions are using the computer to facilitate this process. The students at these schools (and the faculty) are not bounded by the people who are two or three doors down from them or the people they happen to run into. They can leave messages online and get answers back—from people at their school or from folks in other time zones and countries.

I have used electronic bulletin boards in my classes on social issues and technology at both Carnegie Mellon and St. Olaf. Though there is initial apprehension, the students usually think it is a lot of fun. And they learn from each other in an environment in which they can prepare their contributions and carefully consider other's comments. Very often, those students who are most shy in class can interact with skill electronically—perhaps because there are fewer social pressures in online interaction.

Do my students never talk face-to-face? Of course not. In fact in most organizations electronic mail generally augments communication in other modes—it doesn't replace it (Kiesler & Sproull, 1987). That is, if we interact with other people over electronic mail, that's additive communication. It doesn't replace face-to-face communication. People just talk to each other more and, sometimes, about a wide range of topics.

That is one suggestion about how computers might really change education—by allowing peer learning without taking away from regular class time. This use of technology can be implemented with cheap computers and modems—though of course it is better if students can create and send pictures, animation, spreadsheets, and the like.

The urge to get that latest, best technology is understandable, and even commendable. Students need to be prepared for the technology they will meet in the outside world. Unfortunately, we often feel we need "X" technology because it is new and sexy. To avoid this urge, I suggest we establish firm non-technical goals for what we want to do with this neat technology. Once we've determined those non-technical goals, we should insist that they are implemented and we should check up on them regularly. If we do this faithfully, the technology will help us teach rather than frustrate or frighten us.

REFERENCES

Becker, H.J., and C.W. Sterling. "Equity in School Computer Use: National Data and Neglected Considerations." *Journal of Educational Computing Research* 3 (1987): 289-311.

Cuban, L. *Teachers and Machines: The Classroom Use of Technology Since 1920.* New York: Teachers College Press, 1986.

Kiesler, S., and L. Sproull. *Computing and Change on Campus.* New York: Cambridge Press, 1987.

Kraute, R., S. Koch, and S. Sumais. "Computer's Impact on Productivity and Quality of Work-Life: Methodological and Conceptual Difficulties." *Communications of the ACM.* In press.

Rogers, E.M. *Diffusion of Innovations.* New York: Free Press, 1983.

Schonfield, J.W., and D. Verban. "Computer Usage in the Teaching of Mathematics: Issues Which Need Answers." In *Effective Mathematics Teachings*, ed. by D. Grouws and T. Cooney, 169-193. Hillsdale, NJ: Erlbaum, 1988.

Shotton, M.A. *Computer Addiction? A Study of Computer Dependency.* New York: Taylor & Francis, 1989.

Weisband, S. *Interviews with Faculty Software Developers*. Unpublished manuscript, 1986.

Weizenbaum, J. *Computer Power and Human Reason: From Judgment to Calculation*. San Francisco: W. H. Freeman, 1976.

HOW TEACHERS TEACH, HOW STUDENTS LEARN: A SEARCH FOR THE SIGNIFICANT

PAUL LACEY

When I think of my relation to advances in technology I often think of an essay by Robert Benchley in which Benchley describes a friend of his caught in a hotel fire, who rushes down the hall to where there is a glass case holding an ax and a sign saying, "Break and use in case of fire." His friend breaks the case, takes out the ax, then thinks about how to use it. He can chop a hole in his hotel room door thus letting the fire have more fuel, or he could break his window thus giving it more oxygen, but when the firemen rescue him, he's standing in the corner of his room making threatening passes at the flames with the ax.

That's the way I see myself with reference to a whole lot of technology. I should say that I have given up a manual typewriter within the last year for an electric one, making a bold leap into the middle of the twentieth century. In preparing for this, I thought I'd better shadow Bill McKeachie awhile. I took his outline, did some reading, and was particularly helped by the college classroom teaching and learning described in a 1986 research review. Something Bill and his associates say there is that our goals for higher education now go beyond transmitting knowledge to helping students develop cognitive structures, skills, strategies, motivation for continued learning, and problem solving. Those are some important ways for me of expressing goals of higher education.

Lacey is Professor of English, Earlham College, Richmond, Indiana.

I have some others that are not necessarily different in kind, but may be different in expression. One I suspect we all would want to talk about is *liberating*—helping people be liberated from misinformation, from prejudice, from inadequate cognitive structures. Another certainly associated with that is *empowering*, and that turns me to thinking about people's inner-growth, self-reflection, and innovation. A number of people here will undoubtedly recognize that one of the influences in my thinking was the voice of Robert Skolls in regard to textual power. His book suggests that in an age where the manipulation of people by text is so overwhelming, what we should not teach is priest-like submission to text. What we should do is help people learn how to read, interpret, and criticize text to gain power over text and to produce texts of their own.

In some ways the goals and issues facing teachers are complicated, but not fundamentally changed in the long run, by greater access to information.

Let me imagine we are now in a situation where there was immediate and unlimited access to information in the study of literature. What would be different? Now the student says to me, "When I did my research last night, I found a lot of sources, but this library doesn't have any of the best ones. May I have an extension?" In the future I can imagine a student saying "When I did my research last night, I found 400 books and articles under the key word indexes, and they are all waiting in the library right now. May I have an extension?" The most obvious issue raised by unlimited access to information is that it becomes very difficult to know what constitutes useful information and even more difficult to figure how information can be patterned into changes and shaped into knowledge.

To point back to Bill's questions, what are the cognitive structures, paradigms, metaphors, which inform what we call information? The best thing about imagining unlimited access to information is that it forces us to give up a fantasy of total control of a field or discipline. It forces us to acknowledge that information, data and facts very often are like other things—opinion and personal experience included—which may help us to dependable knowledge, but alone may not be knowledge. Unshaped, unformed information may even obscure knowledge.

Kenneth Boulding, noting what a great intellectual tool/invention social science indexing is, says we gain knowledge through the orderly loss of information. That seems to me a very useful thing to have in mind. At first when we think of all that luscious information just waiting for us to submerge ourselves in we are likely to find it tragic that the human memory and mind are so limited. Freely flowing information always is slowed by that wretched bottleneck. But information certainly is not knowledge, until human minds receive it, shape it, reflect on it, rework it, and hand it on with something like respect and good will to other human beings for them to contribute their parts of the process.

We really are not the obstacle. We are the makers of information, we are the reason for information to exist and the source of any informing principle. Let me trace out some implications of what I'm saying by thinking a few minutes about a course I'll teach next term over the British romantic period. The course will be for people in the middle of the English major. I can presume everyone shares some introductory experiences, some common texts to use for comparison, some elementary experiences with what critics do, and recognition that one way to study literature is to historicize it, putting works in their time frame. But there are other ways to approach literary study by genre, by theme, by variety of critical schemata, which repudiate other approaches.

What can and should one hope to accomplish with the course? I will suggest a few of the larger goals, then some specific activities. I want people to learn how to pay attention to a text, to focus on it and to frame questions that bring us closer to the work. In the process of seeking answers, I want us to learn how to revise, refine, or replace our questions. I want us to do that in company with other readers and framers of other questions—not only the people in the room, but everybody else we can imagine who has ever thought about these questions of these texts. I want us to research, to search again. I like to connect that with the etymology of *respect*, which is to look again, to research, to respect. C.S. Lewis says, "An unscholarly person may be defined as one who reads books only once." I want us to listen to things more than once. I want us to learn how to hear a particular voice clearly, discerning it from other voices, learning to hear and recognize a variety of distinct voices—including one's own and of companions in the classroom, then of companion questioners, wherever we start finding their voices.

I want us to learn to frame answers to the questions we've raised and to do that in conversation with others. I would like us to learn how to make these and similar steps into a recurring and self-reflective action. I want, in the process of looking at and valuing text, to advocate collaborative learning and what Erik Erikson calls a style of fellowship. Those are some of the things I want to work on. Any of you who've been thinking about this immediately sees some of the problems for my discipline and probably for yours: In addition to familiar issues of canons, canonomical methods, standards of judgment, and assessment of evidence, how do you learn to listen clearly to one voice and avoid silencing some other voices that might be heard?

Recalling that Romantic period course next term, what can and should one hope to accomplish? First of all, more of the same. More historicizing, more text for comparison, more writing experiences. The course repeats such things to reinforce procedural knowledge of students, to give them more experience and confidence, and to extend their limits of what is familiar in the ways we can find to talk to each other, the vocabulary we can understand together, the questions we hold in common and that are unique. The course ought to do some new things as well, to raise new questions about familiar and unfamiliar text.

What makes a literary period? Can we study a literary period the way geologists study geological periods? People in literature seem to want to advocate or repudiate literary periods. You loved the metaphysical and are therefore expected to disparage if not dislike the Romantics. You hate the Augustinians, so you probably like the Romantics. You adore the moderns, some literary people use language like that. You admire the contemporary, but you reject post modernism. Literary people seem to take literary periods very much to heart. Do geologists say they adore the Ordovician, regret the Pliocene and really relate to the Neolithic? Well, not around the rest of us anyway. I don't know what they do when they have had three beers together.

All this reminds us that additional goals in literature courses, which have their counterparts in many other areas of study, have to do with knowing and understanding, with the feelings as well as the intellect. Learning what touches and moves one in literature is trying to account for why one is so moved or touched.

It's learning to extend the range of one's sympathies and pleasures along with ones increased mastery over text and other forms of information. All of this work may require structuring a course so we scrupulously avoid a lot of extra information at certain points.

These are some of my goals. How should I organize the course? We have 10 weeks, four class hours each week, and whatever I can find it reasonable to expect in the way of work outside class. Let us remember that information may be unlimited in access but time and energy are not. What shall I require as readings and why? What shall I require as activities and why? How shall I orchestrate readings, discussions, writings, and other activity to achieve as many of the goals as I can? How shall I leave room to incorporate my students' goals for the course? How can I best affirm those goals or challenge them? That seems necessary. How can I evaluate and respond to the work of students so our goals may be fulfilled and perhaps new ones emerge? Notice, a lot of those questions will help shape the information I decide to require for the commonality of experiences that must underlie such a course. Commonality is a restricting principal, but a necessary one.

If I have my way, we'd start by reading lyrical ballads. We would do it without the intervention of any critical or historical notes. We would ask one another what we notice about a book that is a 1798 contemporary of ours. We'd ask what we notice, why we notice it, what our first responses to the poems are, which ones we like, which are uninteresting or unlikable to us, and why. What do the poems remind us of, what do they recall, because they are so different from what we are used to. Do the poems and the author's preface of 1798 make us aware of repetitions, variations on image, theme, idea, attitude? Can we imagine anything about these poems that is most likely to be the result of having been written nearly 200 years ago? Those questions and others like them could easily lead on to wide ranging searches of a literature about the period, but our first work would be framing questions, exploring issues, which look interesting and rich for increasing our understanding of those texts and other texts we are using for comparison and of our own tastes and concerns of readers of literature. Framing questions leads on to developing methods of study, search strategies, ways to study collaboratively.

What constitutes useful or significant information for the course gets defined as we go along—as we entertain questions, as we choose what is worth our while in terms of curiosity or pleasure to spend more time on. All this limits what will be information for the purposes we are following and if we acknowledge that, we are still on reasonably safe ground; if we acknowledge that this is not the last word—but the first word or the middle of a conversation—we are still on safe ground. There are difficulties in approaching the study this way. One is that it may not be self-reflective enough. Canons deserve to be challenged, but they exist to identify some commonalties of experience and a course of study. They therefore have the defects of their virtues. So opening up to alternative images, metaphors, models, examples, maybe new canons, will be very important. But we will not even pretend to be able to be open to all alternatives in 10 weeks, four hours a week.

One of the things that the information explosion has done is to make us give up the pretense we can cover everything. So we try to sample approaches, alternative questions, being explicit that this sampling is intended to allow us to recognize that figure and ground do not have to stay in an unchanging relationship. So in this course I order a work that offers contexts for the period—the religious, political, economic climate of the times, the activities in the arts and sciences. Another work may follow themes of consciousness in the age, thus stressing a century of psychological approaches to the key worth. Then as I was doing this course last year—a week before the course was to begin—I got an announcement about a new book. I immediately sent off for it and put it on reserve. We will use it more substantially this year, *Feminism in Romanticism*, an essay collection, which challenges the canon, which challenges the critical approaches that have been standard for years, which raises adversarial questions on some of these texts.

I choose all of those, plus a single anthology, despite my dislike of anthologies, because that lets me save students some money to spend on other texts. I have constructed a course that frankly acknowledges that there is a wealth of material we are not touching together, material that is waiting for an informing principle or a framing question that can be explored by the student whose questions or commitments make it appropriate to use that additional information at the starting point of knowledge.

When we think of unlimited access to information, we may be excited then fearful. So we start creating prolegomena, prefaces, propaedeutics, or heuristics. Is everybody's favorite word in there?

There are things you have to do before you are allowed to do the thing you're going to do. These things may be both essential and appropriate, but those all are channels that we then start creating to which we can narrow and focus all that material. As I say, that may be both essential and appropriate. It may also be, however, that we make it possible for ourselves to live with the fear of too much data by being more reflective about what knowledge is and how we can turn information, opinion, and experience into knowledge.

We can from that, I would hope, raise other kinds of questions, which I can only put on the table. How does knowledge connect with power? How does knowledge connect with wisdom? How is it possible to move from information to knowledge to wisdom in the course of learning and studying? What steps can a course offer along that way? What steps can a course only acknowledge raising the questions about, leaving answers, and ways to get answers to all of us in the group?

It seems to me that if we think about those kinds of issues in relation to the information explosion, we don't have to be terrified there will be unlimited access. We do have to worry that we do not close off access because we don't know how to handle things; but if we are frank in saying that we handle what we can and stand ready to respect what others can handle, we are engaged in the middle of a conversation, the middle of experiencing things together, and that what comes into that must somehow inform us and be informed by our questions and our experience. Then we have no reason to fear.

HOW TEACHERS TEACH, HOW STUDENTS LEARN: THE EXCITEMENT OF DISCOVERY

MARY STURGEON

What are some of the problems peculiar to the teaching of art history? The main tools that concern art historians are pictures of all kinds of objects. That is to say, we consider objects one step removed from the actual objects themselves, and the monuments differ a great deal. We cover the three major media of painting, sculpture, and architecture, as well as various other works that are often grouped together as the minor arts, like gems, jewelry, glass, and mosaics, and in some cases, items of clothing like belts and sandals. Further, one of my studio colleagues makes neon sculpture, so there is quite a variety of materials to consider.

For teaching purposes the field of art history is divided into areas through a variety of means. Historical division is primary, followed by geographical origin, medium, artist, and subject. In the teaching of art history, apart from the conveyance of information about works of art and their historical and social context, a major concern is teaching methods of analysis. We must teach students who come from various backgrounds, many of them never having seen a work of art before, how to deal with questions of style—how to recognize, how to describe, how to proceed to the analysis of styles, whether styles of a broad era, a narrower historical period, or a geographical region. We want them to come out of a class, for instance, in Classical Art, excited not only about the actual monuments that they have been learning about, but about being able to visit a museum with a friend (here is a good way of using "peer

Sturgeon is Professor of Art History, University of North Carolina, Chapel Hill, North Carolina.

learning") and explain some of the artwork to the friend regardless of whether they have studied every object or not, because they have learned a way of looking. They have learned how to see, how to analyze with their eyes, how to deal with questions of composition and how to analyze what makes up a work of art. They have learned how to consider questions such as: what is the importance of line in this object, what is the importance of form, how is color value changed from one side of a painting to another, what are the contrasts of light and shade, what makes something recognizable as coming from the Renaissance or Baroque periods.

Introductory courses often begin with a sharp contrast of black versus white, that is, the Archaic versus the Classical period, or the Renaissance versus Impressionism. We proceed from there to increasingly finer distinctions.

There are various modes of analysis in art history. I have mentioned the analysis of style. Art historians tend to fall into groups depending upon whether they are stylistically oriented or oriented in other directions. Traditions of subject matter or iconography presents another approach, as does attribution to artist or connoisseurship, which results from distinction of fine details and the manner of rendering particular features of a human being, like eyes, ears, hands, or feet. We are also interested in technique, the development of technology in the ancient world, as distinct from more recent times, and the relation of the art object to its social context and to religion. So this is a very broad field. That's why I find it exciting. That's why students find it an interesting major.

Students of art history are varied. That is most true at the introductory level. They come to us initially in relatively large survey classes with 160 to 200 people. I think of that as large, but my introductory psychology course at the University of Minnesota had 2,000 students. I was told that it did not matter because we were hearing the best people in the department, which made me feel rather small and unimportant. We try to counteract this (inevitable) effect by dividing the class into discussion sections with teaching assistants. A lot of peer learning goes on in the halls as well.

On a more advanced level, the variety of student is not as great, but I have always felt it was important to find out in the first class who they were and what their backgrounds were. There might be a mixture of art history majors and studio art majors, people concerned with painting and sculpture who have little historical background, together with students who have had a lot of courses in classical languages or ancient history but never a visual course before.

Students bring to the classroom a tremendous variety of backgrounds, to all of which I must speak. I will never forget the time at Oberlin in my first or second year of teaching when I mentioned Homer and asked, "Is there anybody here who doesn't know who Homer was?" Well, several hands went up, rather hesitantly, and a lot of other people sat on their hands. Ever since then I've been well aware that it is good to define those things that "most people" know just so the person who doesn't know them and is afraid to ask will learn from that and carry it on with him. I tend to find that such variety in students' backgrounds makes for an exciting classroom, provided one can create a relatively warm atmosphere, one that is open to questions so discussions develop in different directions, depending on the areas students would like to investigate further.

What happens to our majors? Some follow a rather tradition-al route. In the past many went to graduate school and pursued careers in teaching. I would say that is a relatively small number these days, which seems just as well considering the job market. Others have found alternative ways of using their major. Some go into the museum world, becoming registrars and curators in university and public museums. There is also increasing emphasis on the development of educational programs in museums. It is often a delight to give a lecture at a major museum, as I did this fall at the Walters Art Gallery in Baltimore, and find that there are multiple education programs in process, each of which was not only well attended, but sustained participants interest for the entire day.

A former major from Oberlin went to Princeton for his Ph.D. in art history and became a dealer in the art market, which is generally thought of as "the trade." Getting your hands "dirty" in this fashion can be contrasted with doing field archeology, the other way of "getting your hands dirty." This is also another way of using art history. One is always disappointed initially to find that the brightest member of a class intends to go to law school. Then, you think, maybe we can get him or her interested in becoming a collector or a supporter of the art museum, interested in cultural outreach projects. There are lots of ways of using or maintaining an involvement with the field of art history. In teaching, the constituen-cy is broad. We try to speak as much as possible to its various components, including, one should mention, the museum docents, both those active currently and future prospects.

What are the art history teacher's primary concerns, apart from the general outlines just mentioned? In classroom teaching especially, the quality of the image is important. The artwork is studied through reproductions of it on slides and in photographs. We are constantly searching for better photographs from which to make slides. The quality of the visual image is very important if the original is not available. Many of us live in parts of the United States where there are relatively few original works of art, especially in certain teaching areas, and many students have had little or no museum experience, which makes the quality of the image used in teaching of even greater importance.

At Oberlin College, for instance, I felt very fortunate to have four pieces of Ancient marble sculpture in the college museum, and I would use them in various ways. The University of North Carolina at Chapel Hill also has a museum, as many colleges and universities do. There the Ackland Art Museum pieces prove useful for talks to museum docents, but the collection is not as useful for upper-level undergraduate or graduate teaching.

In the classroom we are teaching people how to see and analyze works of art, as conveyed through slides and photographs. With some media this is not much of a problem. In ancient art, Greek vase painting makes a good example. This forms a part of most introductory courses and is a topic in which I give an advanced course in alternate years. Vases come in various sizes: they range from four to ten inches in height, but can be as much as six feet tall. If they are projected on the screen, they may be enlarged 10 to 100 times, which gives a great advantage in terms of enlarging the details so they will be visible in a classroom of 30 to 150 people. You can show a large number of people the smallest vase much better in the classroom than you can in a museum, where it is difficult for 20 people to see such an object at the same time. It is especially difficult to turn it around because you have to move those 20 people around the case in which the object is located. In museums one is competing also with the acoustics, and the fact that there is frequently another teacher or tour leader "yelling her head off" on the other side of the room is no help. I have done a fair amount of that and it is exciting. It is fun teaching with the originals, but certain kinds of objects pose certain kinds of problems.

With a vase the mode of painting is relatively flat. That is to say it frequently depends on a linear, two dimensional design, and therefore it is a type of art that can be translated into a drawing fairly easily. That brings up one technique that is very useful in teaching art: suggesting that students sketch what they are studying. This does not mean they need to know how to produce a finished drawing, the process of making the sketch helps them understand the object's form and decoration. This technique can help convey what is meant by a two-dimensionally conceived, as opposed to a three-dimensionally conceived, work of art. Vase painting is a medium that lends itself to this procedure.

Marble sculpture is much more difficult to conceptualize because it is in the round. In addition, it is difficult to photograph well. If the sculpture is itself a Roman copy of a Greek statue, the photograph of it is already three steps removed from the original. All of this leads to the question of videodisks, which are yet another step removed from the original object.

The potential that lies in the area of videodisks is very exciting. This is not only because pulling the same slides year in and year out, which I have been doing for nearly 20 years, is exceedingly monotonous. It is nearly the same thirty to forty slides, give or take five or ten, that need to be pulled for each 50-minute class. I would love to have a videodisk that would be organized from the point of view of each course I give. I have consulted the Center for Learning and Teaching at Chapel Hill to see what is on hand, and to look at the catalogs of what is available.

The main problem, and this is why I've spent some time on the importance of the visual image, is that the quality of reproduction of the image, which can vary tremendously depending on the equipment used, is not very good. An unclear or inexact image is the sort of thing that some of my colleagues would reject out of hand, and I have seen them after demonstrations organized by some computer companies walk out of the room in a huff. If the pixels are too large and the image on the screen is not sufficiently refined, it may not be possible to talk about the complex uses of modeling, the contrast of light and shade, or the particular way of rendering, which would allow one to make an attribution to a specific artist. This matters the most for Old Master paintings from the Renaissance and Baroque periods, but it is less critical for relatively flat works of art, two-dimensional objects like graphic plans, architectural plans, pictures of buildings, or some two-dimensional paintings.

I would imagine that there may be a waiting period of roughly five years before the visual image on videodisks reaches an acceptable quality level and the cost of putting it into the classroom is not prohibitive. The idea of the videodisk is certainly very exciting and could be used in the classroom as well as for study purposes. At the moment photographs are posted on brackets in the halls for students to study, and a lot of peer discussion takes place, especially just before exams.

As far as I can determine at Chapel Hill, from asking the Center for Teaching and Learning, there are few faculty who are actually using computers in the classroom for teaching, outside of the Computer Science Department. The most innovative use I have read about, however, is that of an English professor. In his composition courses his students bring in compositions on disks, which he projects on the board, so that the class is able to work on problems of revision, having disassociated the writer from the disk. There do not seem to be many people using computers at the moment, but some are just about ready to become involved. The "Perseus Project," a computer videodisk project organized by Harvard University and Boston University promises to be a useful resource for Classics and Classical Archaeology.

In fields such as my own the new laser technology presents exciting prospects for teaching, but research applications are even more exciting. A number of research indexes now exist "online," including various repertoires of the literature of art, some put out by the Getty Center of Art and some by institutes in France, which are very useful. They have problems, however, especially for a discipline that places great emphasis on historical background. That is to say, retrospective coverage is not yet terribly good. Most such catalogs start with the mid-1970s and that does not help the fields that still value what was said in the late nineteenth century.

There is also a lack of good coverage of current titles. If one is working on a book review or trying to help a student write one as a sample problem, it is difficult to find out what has been published in the last two or three years by using such sources. The main bibliographical reference that applies to my work, the *L'Aunee philologique*, covers all aspects of Classical Studies. Its American office, based in Chapel Hill, is now producing its copy on computer. Therefore, I have access to the computer information online for 1987, but only for American titles. That does not help me as much as it might, but it points to an area in which we may hope for great improvement. This is one item I have put on my "shopping wish list."

There are also vocabulary problems with running searches. Art historians are rather inconsistent in the way they refer to things and the problems are compounded by the vocabulary used by different languages. For instance, there are some subject indexes that are coming out now that have great applicability, but one of their problems is the standardization of vocabulary. This is true in studies of architecture, but even more so in sculpture and painting. The increased use of the computer in this way has made such differences more noticeable and may ultimately lead to a regularization of vocabulary and spelling that will cross language boundaries.

Certainly we need many more subject indexes. I asked one of my colleagues what she would put on her "wish list"; she said she would like to be able to punch into a computer to produce a list of all the paintings produced in 1800 by women artists on a given subject: for example, bathers, women looking out a window, or whatever. I don't think that use of the computer is too far in the future, but at the moment we are moving a little slowly in that direction.

Another way computer technology will be extremely useful is in organizing slide libraries. This is already well advanced, especially on some campuses, like the University of Texas. At the University of North Carolina, for instance, the index to manuscript slides is now on computer. Why is such an index necessary? There must be 20 drawers filled with slides of manuscript illuminations. They are filed by their collection name and inventory number (i.e., Oxford 23.006) and if you happen to remember the manuscript's number, that's fine. Or, if you wrote it down last year when you were putting your course notes together, that's fine. But if this is not your primary field and you would just like to present a manuscript, which you may know by a conventional name, for purposes of comparison, then you need an index.

There are five book-size indexes that we have used previously, but the computer accesses the information much more quickly. The same problem exists in the way the slide filing works in other areas as well, where a subject index will provide a way of sorting through iconographical problems. Colleagues from the classics department have come to me at the end of their rope saying, "I just want to find a vase representation of Heracles Standing with Lion's Skin or Fighting the Amazon or something, but they are filed by artist, city, and according to the museum building that they are in. Of course, that is the way Greek vase painting as a subject is organized, but a person teaching Greek Mythology courses would organize the material by subject. So that is another area in which a variety of online indexes would be most useful.

Another way of doing research or helping students with research problems is in making attributions. I mentioned earlier that artists differ in the way they render individual details, such as eyes, ears, nose, and throat (it sounds like certain kinds of doctors), or hands and feet, and this is true particularly in certain periods. I asked my colleague who teaches American art what his great computer "wish list" would consist of and he said, "I want to see eyes, a series of eyes, all made in the same period, so that I can start to work on an artist whose work I am not familiar with, someone that I may have just discovered in a North Carolina local collection, and present it to the computer. The computer will come up with six very similar eyes by such and such an artist made at certain times, and I will go on from there." In other words, such a database would allow for a means of searching through the discipline, simplifying, and certainly saving a lot of time and effort in putting together a certain kind of search. This would be applicable to the study of Greek vase painting, in which a small detail like the mode of rendering the human ear can provide a basis for attribution. In some cases these may resemble curled macaroni or tortellini.

I am interested in the prospect of the interactive videodisk. This magical concept, therefore, I have put on my "shopping list." Articles in art library newsletters indicate that a number of museums in this country, the Boston Museum of Fine Arts, the Philadelphia Museum of Art, Modern Museum of Art, and the Metropolitan Museum of Art, have formed a consortium to make a pilot disk designed for educational use, which will feature Impressionist and post-Impressionist paintings. It is probably aimed, as are most videodisks coming out, at the high school-to-adult level. This is a start, and this is very promising.

Last week an advertisement arrived from the Louvre for a series of three videodisks, one of which will be devoted to the antiquities of Egypt, the Near East, Greece, and Rome. One question to be asked is: if an object is published only on such videodisks like this, what is the proper way of referring to it in a scholarly publication, and what effect is that going to have on the scholar-teacher who works in an institution where such disks are not available? We are just beginning to cope with these problems, which will presumably be worked out relatively quickly.

I have a few views about the problem of students' unlimited access to information; these views are different from those already expressed at this forum. From one vantage point, there are very few limits on students' access to information at the moment. If you consider the fact that many college libraries are closed Friday and Saturday nights and Sunday mornings, which can often be annoying to a faculty member, one might point out that this is seldom the focus of student unrest. Few students really seem to take full advantage of current opening hours.

Second, the prospect of students discovering information previously unknown to a faculty member ought to be exciting, not daunting. In nearly 20 years of teaching, it has seldom occurred that a student working on a research project has brought me an object or an article that I have not seen before, but this happened last fall. I thought it one of the most exciting things that had happened in a long time. Not only had I not seen the particular object, but it didn't resemble anything else I knew of, and it did not fall into an obvious category, which was intriguing. I found the situation very refreshing and one that made the student's project that much more interesting to consider.

I think those of us who are really involved with the problems of our disciplines enjoy teaching because of the kinds of reactions and interest we get from students, because of the joy one gets in that moment when the classics major really understands how to analyze a picture, or when the studio artist finally comes to grips with putting a work of art into a historical framework. Those moments are what keep us going and why most of us are here. I look forward to more in the future and hope that we can, through helpful coaching, help eliminate the problems of the information "glut" for students. I hope we can focus students' attention on those problems and methods of analysis that are most significant, which will help them to move ahead, but also help us to grow in productive ways as teachers.

HOW TEACHERS TEACH, HOW STUDENTS LEARN: MAKING TEACHERS LESS LIKE PRIESTS AND STUDENTS MORE LIKE TEACHERS

JERRY WOOLPY

I will discuss two ways students use technology to take control of what they learn and thus improve their rate of return on effort. Like the best teachers, the right technology helps students take more responsibility in the learning process.

The first application of technology is a computer managed instruction program called Delphi, which I have worked on for the past 15 years. The program harnesses the computer to handle files of essay questions and answers. The files consist of questions students have asked, answers given one another's questions, and commentaries they provide each other's answers. In biology, political science, and literature, or other classes where Delphi is used—on Monday, for example, after students have completed a reading assignment or listened to a lecture, they enter questions about the material into the Delphi computer files; Wednesday, they answer each other's questions drawn at random from the pool that were entered Monday; then on Friday, they comment on and evaluate each other's answers. Without the teacher having to read all of the questions and answers, students get regular exercise in writing, thinking, and thorough feedback from at least three randomly selected classmates participating in the weekly review.

Woolpy is Professor of Biology and Psychology, Earlham College, Richmond, Indiana.

Unlike much computer assisted instruction, Delphi supports considerably more than associative learning. Students have to express complex ideas in terms that are intelligible to other students. The structured student dialogue informs subsequent class discussions, improves writing and can be adopted in existing courses without substantial revision. It doesn't take the amount of teacher preparation time that most educational software requires, either. While typical educational software takes hundreds of hours of preparation for each hour of instruction, Delphi can be set up for a course in 30 minutes and provide hundreds of hours of instruction. Where other programs give added control to the computer and the teacher, Delphi is a more efficient and better learning device in giving control to the students.

Using Delphi, students ask the same kinds of questions that instructors would ask, perhaps with more insight and certainly with a closer perspective of what is novel and interesting about the material from a student viewpoint. Like teachers, they have to decide what is important, what is correct, and what is of good quality. Eventually they realize there may be various good answers to good questions.

The second application of technology also gives students more control and responsibility for their own learning and makes them more like teachers. They do this by use of the library—not the brick building in the center of the campus—but the library of the world's literature. The library is a great equalizer for students because it offers all of the information that is published.

We teach introductory students that biology, unlike some disciplines, has a highly organized conceptual framework that is always growing and changing. Because of this, last year's notes have to be revised and supplemented. In fact, even last month's notes may be obsolete. But it isn't easy to know what to read because there may be thousands of citations on a particular topic published in a short time. Nevertheless, scientists have developed a process of publication contingent upon favorable peer review. This system together with a knowledge of the hierarchy of journals helps guide the selection of what to read and how much stock to put in it.

On the first day of an introductory course for science and non-science majors, we explain that information about biology obtained from television, radio, newspapers, and magazines may not be accurate. These sources provide a good way to learn what is being discovered, but the information should be confirmed and expanded by reference to the professional literature. We teach introductory students how to locate and read this literature. This is done by giving them the kinds of questions to answer that might be asked of a doctoral candidate. The difference is that the doctoral candidate would be expected to answer immediately from memory, while our students are given one week and access to the library.

Here is an example of a question: "Under what circumstances would you expect to find conifers versus hardwoods in a temperate forest in Michigan or Wisconsin? Why are there pine trees or why are there oak trees in a particular forest?" Biologists have speculated about this and there is data available to consider. But the question does not have an easy answer. The student begins research with the textbook, dictionaries, and encyclopedias. Then secondary sources are consulted; these are articles and books that summarize and interpret data collected by others. Finally, students learn enough about the problem to be able to find and read primary articles, sources presenting original data collected by the authors and accepted for publication by other scientists. They use these to write a three- to five-page essay answering the question, documented with at least five citations of primary sources.

"Under what circumstances and to what extent are pastoral peoples more efficient farmers and better conservationists than agriculturalists?" is another example. Many of our students are vegetarians who are convinced that to be otherwise is always inappropriate (if not immoral). We don't attempt to change their nutritional habits, but we try to help them inform themselves about some realities of empirical human ecology.

When they answer these kinds of questions they become expert. They experience the power of knowing what is known. After this reformation, their learning is no longer bound by interpretations of their teachers and textbooks. In subsequent courses we build on this experience with additional library work: 1) reviewing the sources of key articles to check the reliability of authors' accounts, 2) developing research proposals for projects designed to test hypotheses about phenomena on the frontiers of biology, and 3) checking publication records of faculty at schools they are considering for graduate training.

As the technology for locating information improves, our current emphasis on bibliographic instruction is becoming somewhat trivialized. This is because it is now easy to access the latest information. As a result we should spend more time with the primary literature and less on how to find it. The real revolution occurred with the advent of *Science Citation Index* over 25 years ago. What is likely to happen from now on is the gradual recognition of the power that information technology makes available to us all. This should make the content of science education less and less close-ended. Hopefully technology (like Delphi and the library) will make teachers less like priests and students more like teachers.

HOW TEACHERS TEACH, HOW STUDENTS LEARN: "DOING" HISTORY AND OPENING WINDOWS

RICHARD HUME WERKING

A few months ago one of our chemistry professors at Trinity mentioned to me that his students sometimes had to stop "doing chemistry in the laboratory" to go to the library to access the chemistry literature. In response to my leading question, he quickly agreed that using the library was not the same as "doing chemistry"; that was done in the laboratory.

The situation is quite different in history, especially in my own sub-discipline, American history. Several years ago, William Appleman Williams, dean of the infamous "Wisconsin School of American Diplomatic History," published an engaging piece in the Organization of American Historians *Newsletter*, "Thoughts on the Fun and Purpose of Being an American Historian."

To Williams the library *is* the laboratory of the historian and the history student. As he put it in his article, he always sends "undergraduates as well as graduate students off into the bowels of the library to read other people's mail."[1] Williams also made an explicit comparison between learning history and learning chemistry, quoting a chemistry major in his senior seminar in foreign policy: "I never knew [before that] I could do history like I do silicon crystals. You got me into something new; you put a new window in my head. There's no formula for this one. I get to write my own equations. And, man, that is fun."[2]

Werking is Associate Professor of History and Director of the Library, Trinity University, San Antonio, Texas. In May 1991 he will become Librarian, Associate Dean, and Professor of History at the United States Naval Academy, Annapolis, Maryland.

What did Williams mean when he wrote about "doing history?"

For the most part, you are involved in reading and interpreting documents, and placing those documents within a context of questions that interest you, while simultaneously being willing to confront surprises which cause you to see a richer and more complex context. This can occasionally involve, though usually at a graduate student level, finding important new documents that other historians have not seen. Much more commonly among undergraduates as well as graduate students, it takes the form of viewing familiar documents in an unfamiliar way. For upper-division undergraduates, it is also important to me that they confront what scholars have said about these issues.

As a teacher of history off and on for more than 20 years, my aim has been to get students to ask important and informed questions about aspects of our past, and to get them to offer some tentative answers to those questions. In addition to things I tell them in lecture or during discussion, I also have them come into contact with other points of view via assigned readings (whether on reserve or purchased by them), or by more open-ended assignments like book reviews or papers. I believe in including open-ended assignments because I don't want to spoon-feed my students by serving directly or indirectly as the source of all their information in a given course; I want them to acquire some of the skills necessary to turn up information on their own, so they not only examine evidence, but also seek and find some of the evidence themselves.[3] I think it is even more important that students encounter documents contemporary to a given time period, such as newspaper and magazine articles; congressional hearings; various research collections on microfilm or microfiche; and other primary sources, such as memoirs. Several students in my upper-division seminar on recent U.S. history have made the 80-mile trip to Austin to use governmental and personal papers at the LBJ Presidential Library.

I suppose that my teaching of history has been guided by a philosophy that's well and briefly articulated by Russell Edgerton, president of the American Association for Higher Education. Edgerton says, "We measure [I'd modify this to say that at least we should measure] our success as educators and our success as educational institutions on the basis of the quality of the encounters we arrange."[4]

In case some of you are wondering why I've been spending so much time talking about the philosophy and some of the details involved in my teaching of history, I want to quote from a wonderful little book by MIT historian Elting Morison, *From Know-How to Nowhere: The Development of American Technology.* "We can now build machines that will do almost everything for us," Morison writes.

> The task at hand is to design and control things so that the...surrounding we create for ourselves will serve our interest better than the supplanted...environment did....The criteria for...design and control cannot be established by a search for the maximum potential in each particular machine or system—how better to cool a room; how more easily to blow up some part of the world we do not at the moment want. The criteria must derive from some general scheme that all the parts and pieces can fit into and serve. Such a scheme cannot be based only on our knowledge of what machines can be built to do, which is almost anything. It has to be grounded in the sense of ourselves as the governing reference point....Frankenstein ingeniously came up with a marvelous creation, and it did him in—because he hadn't thought through what he wanted to do with it.[5]

Now what changes do I see in the next few years in my teaching and that of my colleagues? That's hard to say for certain. One point to stress is that faculty are quite conservative, history faculty being among the most conservative. Maurice Glicksman, provost at Brown, noted in 1986 that technology has not had a major impact on teaching, and that many faculty have no desire to change their teaching approach.[6] One example in my field, which bears Glicksman out, is the general underutilization by history teachers—and thus by history students—of microfilmed newspapers, periodicals, and research collections, a "new" technology of document delivery that has been around for several decades.

Like Glicksman's faculty, at present I see no reason to change my basic approach to teaching, although I do want to know more about how my colleagues elsewhere do it. Let me give you examples of those assignments that will likely reflect considerable continuity with what teachers do now. One assignment, which I've given several times, is to have students write a book review and in the process to identify, locate, and read four or more published reviews of the same book, and then weave into their own review essay some important points raised by other reviewers. In the future this assignment will likely be carried out much as it is presently; perhaps the several book review indexes and abstracts will be on a single disk, maybe along with a few reviews. Hence there may be a modicum of convenience, but not a great deal.

Another assignment, which I developed at the University of Mississippi when I was there for four years, was to have students find an article and an editorial in the *New York Times* in 1962 (via that newspaper's excellent index) about the integration of the university (during which two people were killed), and to compare the account and opinion offered by the *Times* with those in an article and editorial from a Jackson, Mississippi, newspaper of the same time. It was an assignment that had a special impact on Ole Miss students only a decade and a half after the turmoil, as you can imagine, but it's also one that I've found is quite transferable to other colleges. This too is an assignment that is likely to continue much as it has, although the *Times* Index will probably be on disk at some point. I doubt the *Times* itself will be on disk, at least for the years before automated typesetting, nor do I think it especially needs to be. I doubt even more that newspapers with more local readerships will be converted into machine-readable form. Hence students will probably still be finding a particular reel of microfilm and getting it onto some sort of machine in order to confront a document and the issues it raises.

As I noted, my students make extensive use of primary sources to write a major paper. This is probably the sort of relatively open-ended assignment Williams gives his students when he sends them into the library. That these sources will be digitized also is unlikely. But because of the kind of microfilming being aggressively carried out by several firms, many research collections are becoming more widely available.

In short, I think there will be relatively little change in terms of assignments I have used for years. But what is likely to change is that I'll probably be doing some new things I had never thought about doing, or had thought about but didn't know how to accomplish.

One assignment I'll likely give my students within a very few years will compel them to interact with machine-readable records. The federal government, in particular, has created thousands of computer data sets, as described in another issue of the Organization of American Historians *Newsletter*. One example from this article is the following:

> Diplomatic historians and other foreign policy analysts...can benefit from a variety of computer records which are not based on earlier paper series records. One group contains hundreds of public opinion surveys conducted around the world since the early 1950s for the United States Information Agency. The data from hundreds of surveys trace the evolution in foreign support for American foreign policy, and provide evidence of the issues about which the USIA sought foreign opinion. Some specific topics are stationing American troops and nuclear weapons in Europe and the relative strengths of NATO and the Warsaw Pact.[7]

I already envision the outline of an assignment that has students comparing the USIA data on various topics with assessments of foreign public opinion on those topics in contemporary newspapers and opinion journals, and also with what historians and political scientists have had to say about those issues, as well as using the survey itself as a source revealing the concerns of American foreign policymakers.

Another opportunity—which optical disk and hypercard are already beginning to provide—involves visual images. For many years I've wanted to do more with video, to help students observe historical actors and their settings, so that when they subsequently read they'll be better able to visualize. In my seminar on the post-World War II United States, I make use of short documentaries on the various presidents and other major figures like Senator Joseph

McCarthy, to help students see and hear them as well as other contemporary footage that's woven in. I've also occasionally used contemporary feature films as primary sources, asking students to deduce things about the times, using the film as a document. (My favorite is *Pride of the Marines,* made in 1945, starring John Garfield and Eleanor Parker; not primarily a war movie, it does an excellent job of setting the stage for the postwar interventionist United States at home and abroad.)[8] It seems as though short video snippets will be available for students, not only to encounter and contemplate, but also to manipulate and work into their own presentations. Just as students for many decades have produced text as part of their assignments, maybe now they can turn out multimedia presentations, and not just for film classes.

A third type of assignment, which I could do an unsatisfactory version of now, involves maps. My hunch is that via some medium which utilizes computer graphics it will be easier and more interesting for students to tackle substantive map assignments, especially involving variables that change over time—such as population concentration and dispersion (including ethnic composition), patterns of disease or voting, transportation networks, densities of manufacturing and mercantile activity, and so on.

In sum, the next 10 to 15 years of our future will contain important elements of continuity, as well as interesting new opportunities. Much of today's information landscape will not be so much supplanted by new technology as supplemented by it. Some opportunities probably won't be pursued because of faculty conservatism and also because of considerable unevenness in the ability of different institutions to pay for parts of the new technology.

Still, there is no question in my mind that many of us history teachers will be confronting more information resources that are available for our work, in a much greater variety of formats. I'm going to need to be even more of a coordinator, helping arrange my students' encounters with the resources they need to do history. Some of these I'll supply (via bookstore or reserve or my own bookshelves), others I'll refer them to specifically, and still others I'll expect them to encounter on their own—and I may not in some cases know that these pieces exist. The last happens fairly frequently now and doubtless will increase. And that's fine with me.

A problem I foresee is that some professors, faced with what could appear to be a flood of available resources for teaching, might retreat into the position of providing all the information they think their students will need. Such a retreat could be facilitated by the growing popularity of customized packets of documents pulled together by the faculty member, photocopied by the off-campus copying center, and sold to students at the copying center or the bookstore.

There are at least three developments (two under way and one potential) that might work against such a retreat. One is that via electronic mail and fax machines, faculty who want their students to do history in interesting ways can share ideas, assignments, syllabi, and reading/viewing lists, which will likely encourage those faculty who are at least potentially interested. This is what I meant earlier about wanting to know more about how my colleagues at other institutions structure their courses.

A second possible development occurred to me after conversations with two former students about papers they had written for me. Trinity was hosting the third annual National Conference on Undergraduate Research, the first two having taken place at The University of North Carolina-Asheville. Undergraduates and faculty members were coming from all over the country for the students to present posters and papers reflecting research they'd done. In the process of encouraging my former students to apply as presenters, it occurred to me that these conferences might result in students establishing and maintaining contacts with one another on the basis of mutual research interests. If this happens, wouldn't it be interesting if some of the pressure on faculty to give more substantive assignments and involve students as peers in the learning process might evolve from expressed *student* interest and initiative?

The third and still more institutionalized remedy would be the creation of a national History Education Center, which could serve as a clearinghouse for the sharing of faculty assignments, syllabi, and the like. Such a center could issue a regular newsletter to acquaint college teachers with information about innovative ways of involving students in encounters, both with traditional resources and also with new resources that are becoming available.

So it will be interesting in the next few years to see the extent to which history faculty, and faculty in other disciplines too, embrace the new opportunities. An inhibiting factor will be the significant costs associated with the new technology, but probably not for long. In fact, let me suggest as a concluding observation that it's a good thing that the costs are significant. As Goldilocks would say, they're "just right." The new technology is slowly becoming affordable, and yet costs are still high enough to make us think about what we're doing. Hence faculty, staff, and administrators may be more likely to follow Elting Morison's advice and, avoiding Dr. Frankenstein's error, will think about what they want to do with these new tools—and why.

NOTES

1.   Organization of American Historians, *Newsletter* 13 (February 1985): 3.

2.   *Ibid.*

3.   Jon Lindgren puts it well when he suggests that we view library research "as a quest for evidence to be examined." "The Idea of Evidence in Bibliographic Inquiry," in Cerise Oberman and Katina Strauch, eds., *Theories of Bibliographic Education: Designs for Teaching* (New York: R.R. Bowker, 1982), p.41.

4.   Quoted in Paul G. Pearson, *Powerful Encounters: Defining and Achieving Excellence*, State of the University Address, August 22, 1986 (Oxford, Ohio: Miami University), p.3.

5.   (New York: Basic Books, 1974), pp.3-4, 151.

6.   "Computer Technology and the Three C's of Higher Education," in *Campus of the Future: Conference on Information Resources* (Dublin, Ohio: OCLC, Inc., 1987), pp. 28-29.

7.   Bruce I. Ambacher and Margaret O. Adams, "Utilizing Computer-Readable Records," OAH *Newsletter* 17 (February 1989): 13.

8.   As a graduate student at the University of Wisconsin, I had the good fortune to work as a Teaching Assistant with Professor Paul Glad, who used this technique very effectively in his course on the history of the United States since 1971.

HOW TEACHERS TEACH, HOW STUDENTS LEARN: CONFESSIONS OF A COUNTER-REVOLUTIONARY

GORDON THOMPSON

I probably misunderstood my assignment, but I always do. I thought I got to predict, which humanists rarely get to do, so here goes. Here is my prediction: The response of English departments across the country to the impact of unlimited information access will be the most reactionary, the least imaginative, the most ill-tempered, and the least cooperative of all the academic disciplines. Those of you who, as administrators or librarians, have tried to get English departments to try anything new know that such is our mode of operation under all conditions anyway. We usually find that by denying the future, refusing to cooperate, and holding our breaths until our faces turn purple, we tend to get our way in most things. Our experience with soothsayers serves to justify our behavior.

Twenty years ago, I participated in a conference at which one of the nation's foremost educators announced that within the very near future the three-year degree would be the norm in American higher education. There would no longer be time, we were told, for young people to read all those long novels and epic poems. I was young and credulous, so I started to look for ways to abridge *Heart of Darkness* and "Ode to the West Wind," but my older colleagues said, "Forget it; it will go away," and they kept on assigning *Moby Dick* and *Ulysses* and *Paradise Lost*.

Thompson is Professor of English, Earlham College, Richmond, Indiana.

Ten years ago, I participated in another conference at which I was told that all students would be writing their papers on computers and that English teachers would need to figure out what to teach when misspellings, poor organization, and writer's block were all things of the past. While it is true that nowadays almost all my students write their papers on computers—only future English professors are still using typewriters—I have determined (with scientific precision) that the varieties of compositional wretchedness are exactly what they were before we were given the exciting news about the future.

Today we are told that a revolution is upon us and that facing the revolution is not optional. We are told, furthermore, that the classroom teacher must figure out what to do when we are all freed from print.

Freed from print? The study of literature is not as old as mathematics, philosophy, history, physics. It is the study of print. What we live for is to hold books in our hands. What we teach for is to get others to try it. Some may argue that the study of literature is the study of words, whether spoken, printed, or electronically projected. I suspect that literature is print—or at least words reproduced on a page.

If a revolution really does come to pass, therefore, that frees us all from print, English teachers across the country will probably respond in their customarily constructive way, perhaps by committing hara-kiri in front of their classes. Come to think of it, though, mass suicide would provide presidents and deans with too many free FTEs to devote to technology courses and socially relevant area studies. We will probably just keep on grumbling and assigning *Middlemarch* and *The Iliad*.

Unlike the revolution that was to bring the universal three-year degree and the revolution that promised an end to all split infinitives, however, the revolution of unmanageable information really is upon us. Even English teachers cannot deny this. The issue, then, is how we will respond as teachers.

The brochure that announced this forum tells us that circumstances are going to be so different that they will require an entirely different mind-set. Let me make my position clear: I reject that conclusion utterly. The new circumstances will not require a new mind-set for literature teachers; in fact, they will make the old mind-set more imperative than ever. They will also make the old mind-set harder and harder to maintain. Therein lies the challenge.

The teacher of literature does not deal primarily, or even secondarily, with information. Perhaps we are the only participants in this conference for whom this is true. Our subject matter is texts, especially imaginative texts. Our activity is interpreting and evaluating texts—not gathering information, except such information as helps us interpret and evaluate. As Samuel Johnson put it in the eighteenth century, "What interests the student of literature are works of which the excellence is not absolute and definite, but gradual and comparative; works not raised upon principles demonstrative and scientific, but appealing wholly to observation and experience." The mental qualities we hope to cultivate in ourselves and our students include sensitivity to language, imagination, analytical power, critical judgment, the ability to think historically, and taste.

Today, a student at a small college can measure her reading of *Pride and Prejudice* against 200 other readings—if she has nothing else to do for a semester. In a few years, she will be able to measure her reading against 2,000 other readings—if she has nothing else to do with her life. But the mental qualities she needs will be the same in both cases: sensitivity to language, imagination, analytical power, critical judgment, the ability to think historically, and taste.

The ominous—and exciting—challenge of sudden access to unlimited materials lies in the area of making responsible judgments about what to read. Stated more dramatically, the question is how can we help our students decide what not to read? Right now, we sometimes help students decide what 90 percent of the commentary on a work to ignore. Soon, we will have to help them decide what 99.9 percent of the available commentary to ignore. And this, in turn, is going to exacerbate a problem that exists right now in the teaching of literature.

Most students today are savvy enough to know that the reading and writing of literature are "interested activities." That is, they know that books are written and experienced in cultural contexts, which means somebody's interests are being celebrated at the expense of somebody else's. They know that as Charles Dickens sentimentalizes the poor children of London he is blind to the demeaning images of middle-class women he perpetuates. They know that as Edith Wharton shows us a woman's victimization by old money values in New York she is blind to the anti-Semitism in the portraits of some of her minor characters. They know, in other words, that there is no disinterested literature and there is no disinterested criticism. They know, likewise, that those who claim to be disinterested in the area of literature are the blindest of all. They know that people claim to be disinterested because it is in their interest to do so. Our students believe this because their sociology teachers and their history teachers and their younger literature teachers and their classmates are telling them that it is so. And I, too, believe it is so.

Students now identify themselves as interested advocates in their reading. They announce, for example, "I am a Marxist, and therefore I read Balzac for what he reveals about class conflict." "I am an Afro-American, and therefore I despise Huckleberry Finn." "I am a radical feminist, and therefore I am moved by the poetry of Adrienne Rich." "I am a Jew, and therefore I am deeply offended by *The Merchant of Venice*." "I am an atheist and therefore I cannot find the power in *Paradise Lost*." In other words, students respond to texts in terms of their primary group and ideological affiliations at this point in their lives. This is a problem for the literature teacher because students close themselves off to texts that run counter to their groups' values.

What does all this have to do with unlimited information access? Plenty. Since students will have access to virtually everything and since students will have time to read only the tiniest fraction of the commentaries available to them, who will decide what tiny fraction to read? Who will decide what huge fraction to ignore? You know the answer: ideological groups will decide. The feminist will use a feminist filter on available materials. The gay student will use a gay filter. The Marxist will use a Marxist filter. Every group will publish its guide to recommended commentaries.

Can I blame these students for letting their chosen groups do most of the screening for them? I do precisely that right now. I read those books and articles that my filters tell me are important. My filters, of course, are the prestigious reviewers in my discipline, the ones who solidify their interest and mine. I also follow recommendations of experts who share my political and religious commitments.

The most frightening future, of course, is one in which no one's allegiances will ever be challenged. It is not hard to envision a future in which the vaster the amount of material available to us, the narrower our focus will become. The study of literature will then become an exercise in ideological solidarity and the massaging of preconceptions. We will do nothing to cultivate in our students, sensitivity to language, imagination, analytical power, critical judgment, the ability to think historically, and taste.

Many lovers of literature can be frightened by such a vision of the future because they believe that the literary experience implies a larger, more diversified community. The most important thing about writings of imaginative power, to such persons, is their ability to be shared, to start and sustain conversations. A diverse group of people—yes, ideologically diverse—can construct a reading of a text that is uniquely its own, a reading that is faithful to the text but has the special stamp of that collection of people with their varied interests and commitments. This is why the literature teacher often enjoys teaching the same work to different classes over the years. My guess is that calculus does not change from class to class the way a poem does.

My task, as a teacher of literature to undergraduate students, is to help students come together over a text, to guide them to a shared reading that is the special property of that collection of readers. One of the elements in that shared reading is the research each student does during the course. Will the revolution that this forum anticipates make it easier or more difficult for us to come together during a course? I think it will make it more difficult. In recent years, my literature students have found it more and more difficult to talk to each other. Their differing allegiances and hence their differing researches drive them apart.

To repeat, then, I think this trend is going to continue and unlimited access is going to intensify it mightily. It is not hard to foresee a future in which literary study is more and more isolated, less and less communal. To me, that means literary study that is more and more antithetical to the spirit of literature. It is not hard to conjure up an image of the scholar of the future in his or her workshop, receiving and sending out bits of information that an ideological filter says are acceptable. It is not a kind of scholarship where there is any real conversation, fellowship, judgment, taste, criticism. It is not an image I want to offer to students as an ideal, even as I too share the excitement of having access to all that information.

In spite of all this, I welcome the technological revolution because it will make the old mind-set even more imperative than before. I also think it will make the community implied by writing of imaginative power even more attractive than before. The fellowship that some of us have enjoyed in literary study has been, to some extent, a phony one. It has been overwhelmingly upper and middle class: it has been patriarchal, European, Christian, "scientific." It has depended upon the silencing of many potential participants. The coming together of forthright ideological criticism and unlimited access to all voices will make conversation and community infinitely more difficult—and, potentially, anyway, infinitely more fruitful.

Literature teachers will have to become much more imaginative in finding ways of achieving conversation and community among the non-like-minded. (I am parochial enough to believe that Quaker schools like mine can serve as a model here, with their emphasis on an inner teacher in each individual, their insistence on informality and their tradition of cooperative consensus-seeking.) Literature teachers will need to be much more creative in finding ways to increase sensitivity to language, for students will be bombarded with word usage that is crude, unsuggestive, and inelegant. Literature teachers will need to develop much better exercises than the ones I now use to get students to read outside their areas of ideological allegiance and to distinguish between excellent commentaries and commentaries that are less good.

I expect literature teachers to complain a great deal in the near future. Being literature teachers, we will do it very eloquently. We will lament falling standards and the impersonality of machines. We will deplore the narrowness of every ideology but our own. But I hope we will spend some of our time looking for new ways of preserving some old values and an old mind-set, without which there is really no point in studying literature at all.

HOW TEACHERS TEACH, HOW STUDENTS LEARN: TEACHING IN A BLIZZARD OF INFORMATION

PETER SUBER

For a conference held at my college, I was asked to think about how my teaching—not my research—would be affected by rapid, cheap, and simple access by computer to all the published literature of the human race. Forget what impediments stand in the way of this hypothetical future and imagine that your campus has the means for you and your students to locate, search, sort, copy and store anything in digital form that has ever been in print. How would you answer?

I am a computer enthusiast but, while I find this hypothetical future terribly exciting for research, I do not find it unambiguously good or exciting for teaching. Most of my reservations are not specific to my discipline.

First it is well to admit some of the large advantages.

1. When more full texts are online, we could assign what we wanted without regard to whether it was in print or out of print. Without resort to Kinko's or its competitors, we could assemble a reading list of just the right fragments. Teachers would find new flexibility in designing their syllabi; rich and poor students would find themselves on equal footing for at least one important resource. Even if

---

Suber is Associate Professor of Philosophy and Computer Science, Earlham College, Richmond, Indiana.

the texts we wanted to assign were not online already, we could put them online with a scanner for the cost of a student assistant and royalties. Stevens Institute of Technology did this recently with 2,700 pages of texts by and about Galileo. There will be copyright problems, but they definitely don't belong under advantages.

2. Students already know that they can pursue many topics that interest them by using the library. But some barrier of intimidation prevents many from doing so, even when their curiosity is intense. We may hope that some of the advances in information technology will tear down this barrier and open the doors of knowledge to those who have in effect been waiting outside with longing. I suspect that the evolution of this technology is in the direction of ever greater user-friendliness. However, I can imagine serious ergonomic mistakes that would make the barrier even higher than it is now.

3. Cheap electronic access to information may have a levelling effect on colleges and universities. It cannot make a bad college good, but it can neutralize some of the advantages of a large library or large city. Even if this happens only in a very small degree, small colleges in the country should begin to see more students who would previously have gone to top schools with huge libraries. Mobile faculty will feel more free to live where the quality of life suits their taste and remain fully plugged into the world of their discipline; immobile faculty will have one less grievance.

4. Similarly, there should be less isolation of campuses. Students and faculty should enter a larger intellectual community than just their own institution, and participate in electronic exchanges, dialogs, bulletin boards, and conferences with like-minded peers from all over the world. In the classroom, this will hurt bad teachers who will be more easily exposed; it should help teachers who are on top of things such that no news from the front will discomfit them.

This revolution will deprive the classroom teacher of the license to bluff with impunity, to fall too far behind new developments, and to control students' information and perspective on the subject. It will reward at least one kind of good teacher: the one kind who sincerely desires that students should become intellectually autonomous.

At the same time, the opposite may occur in many places. The universe of available information will be so large that some teachers might actually control their students' command of it the way the mapmaker controls the explorer in the wilderness. But teachers cannot do this simply by scheming to do it; students must allow it to happen by a failure of initiative. I really cannot say whether more students will than will not allow their teachers to exercise this control.

I have as many fears as hopes, most of which could be shared by teachers in any discipline. My discipline is philosophy, and because I teach it in a way that is heavily text-based, I have one fear that could be called provincial—local to disciplines whose work with undergraduates revolves much less around research than around a body of difficult and important texts. Like many teachers of philosophy, literature, classics, religious studies, and history, I assign work that uses the library chiefly to enhance a student's experience of a primary text. So I would use the hypothesized access to information much less and much differently from colleagues in any of the sciences, who require research papers or literature surveys, and even from colleagues in philosophy who focus less on primary texts and more on battles in the journals.

While online texts will permit a new kind of close reading, with multiple windows and fast searches, I fear that an older kind of close reading will fade away. For this purpose, "close reading" is not code for a kind of analysis that some scholars prefer to avoid. It is a consequence of being able to hold a well-produced book in one's hands. Something about the fixity, visual clarity, tactile reality, and even smell, of good books puts students (and me) in the attitude of scholarship. Printed text can be beautiful; it can be a work of craft and art that can be appreciated apart from its content. Books have margins for writing in, personalizing, and appropriating. Printed text can be taken under a tree where there is no electricity, and lingered over long after batteries would expire. Not for a long time will computers be as convenient as a book for random access. Turning back and forth between two pages for comparison (once one has found the two pages) is as fast as one cares to have it, and no command structure and limited windowing capability stand in the way. And it's silent.

I worry that plagiarism would become easier to perform and more difficult to detect. First, there would be more literature more easily accessible from which to steal. Second, there might well be a database specially devoted to term papers. Even now there are commercial cheating services that distribute term papers in hardcopy. Third, the chances would increase that the teacher would not know the source from which the student stole. It is possible, but only after considerable lag-time, that text-search algorithms would be so sophisticated and speedy that plagiarism would become easier to detect by the same technology that made it easier to commit. But the suspicious professor, unless she had a vague idea of the source, would have to search across all the relevant databases, and across all the texts in each.

My largest worry is that more and more students will come to confuse information with education. This worry should be shared across the disciplines. Even if the confusion of information and education does not spread, the glut of easily accessible information will put a new burden on the classroom teacher to make this distinction clear and vivid for students. Today there is barely time in bibliographic instruction to get beyond search strategies to the fine points that permit self-moving scholarship. In the hypothetical future practically all of our bibliographic instruction time will have to be spent on disciplinary methods for *assessing* information and bibliographic leads.

It is possible that my worry is groundless, and that the advent of very wide, very cheap access to huge databases would put information in perspective and lead students to look for the wisdom to appraise and digest it. However, I suspect that this is only a long-term development, at best, and that in the short term the niftiness of it will overwhelm the comparative triviality of it, for many disciplines, and lead almost everyone to overestimate the net gain.

The ultimate question in education, certainly in philosophical education, has never been access to information; it has always been wisdom or the capacity to judge information and build knowledge and action from it. Access is crucial, however, for almost all the sub-ultimate goals of education, including the important political goals for wide and roughly equal distribution of resources. When we get real access, and get the mother lode, we are likely, temporarily, to make the secondary goals of education primary and forget that the primary goal is not served by our new darling.

I worry that there will be a proliferation of junk databases—a difficult category to define, since one person's propaganda is another's writ, and one person's scholarship is another person's ideology. It will be in the interest of each cult and movement to have its own database, just as it will be in the interest of every valid micro-specialization of research. How will students distinguish a large database of literature on creationism from one equally large on super-conducting ceramics? It is very easy for students to think that, if only one were interested in these esoteric subjects, good information is at hand, and that every pile of citations is as reassuring as every other. If students know that creationism is unscientific, or controversial, they might be armed with useful doubts; if they don't, they are liable to serious deception. How will students evaluate a database on European history, with no give-away title, that happens to be thick with articles denying that the holocaust occurred and remarkably thin on the contrary position?

Students who are not already educated in a field cannot distinguish the wheat from the chaff in the databases in that field, but will frequently think that they can or that it is not necessary. There will be online guides to databases offered by the same cults and movements. Students already assume too hastily that access to information is the passport to objectivity, not realizing that ideological divisions differentiate the "information," requiring it to be judged before it can be made useful. They will have the same problem with the diversity of databases that they have today with the diversity of journals. The belief that "if it's in print, it must be true" will give way to the belief that "if it's online, it must be true."

One solution, tempting at first glance, is to avoid specialty databases and stick to the biggest "standard" databases for a given field. However, this overlooks the presence of good material in small databases, and of bad material in the major databases. Students would have the impression that the "standardness" of the major databases somehow vouches for the literature they contain. This is false and misleading. Standard journals publish articles of varying quality and varying ideological perspectives; standard databases stir the pot further by including *journals* of varying quality and varying ideological perspectives.

There are two problems here that are important to keep distinct. First, there are honest disagreements among scholars, usually traceable to prior methodological differences. Each "school" or "paradigm" has its own journals now, and may well have its own databases soon. Second, there are the junk databases. For present purposes it does not matter whether a firm distinction between these categories can be sustained. Nor need we impugn the good faith of writers in the second category. For in a large country there are undoubtedly honest astrologers, anti-semites, and Ph.D. researchers who think that smoking is harmless or that women are congenitally less able than men in mathematics. But when they promote their views in the "marketplace of ideas," and when the marketplace moves onto every desktop, then they set a task for the classroom teacher who wants to empower students to recognize and reject pseudo-science and pseudo-objectivity.

I certainly prefer that all literature should be available than that it should be controlled, even by scholars whom I personally get to nominate. In one sense, it is all available today, and controlled only by the difficulty of using a library. When it is online, this control will lift, and the fake blessing of objectivity associated with computers will touch all of it. So we will experience the problems of naive and indiscriminate citation more then than now. That is not a ground for resisting the advent of information access; it is a call to teachers to watch the scene and anticipate a problem.

The aura of objectivity associated with computers will undoubtedly decay as the next generation grows up. But as long as the aura exists, it will impose a task on teachers to demystify computers. This is one reason why I worry about the influence of online information more than the influence of the same information in print libraries. But even for the next generation, as familiar with computers as we are with the banalities of television, this worry cannot entirely lift. For today's students, raised with print information, do not distinguish among professional journals until they are taught to do so, and are still naive in their deference to judgments that find their way into print.

I worry that bibliographic instruction will overlook the potential for confusing information and education, and will one-sidedly lead students to glory in the riches available to them. The problem will be ignored if library use, bibliographic instruction, information access—whatever one wishes to call it—is conceived as technical training in computer use, database dialing, search commands, and the mysteries of keywords. It will also be ignored if it proceeds by universal rules, independent of disciplinary methods and differences. If non-disciplinary techniques sufficed beyond the most elementary level, then good librarians, simply using good librarianship, would be able to judge all work in all disciplines.

My discipline does not gather or process information in any usual sense. For it, cheap, total, and instant access to the world's literature is definitely secondary to the serious encounter with challenging theory, argument, and vision. But this is true of most disciplines, even those with much more use than philosophy for the technology of information processing. The qualities of mind taught in my discipline, and in the other disciplines traditionally grouped among the liberal arts, including the physical sciences, will be needed more than ever to preserve a clear sense of the primary objectives of education, with all their terrible human difficulties and complexity, in the face of the increasingly spectacular secondary services. When teaching is hard and information access is easy, we will have to give more energy than we give now to focus our efforts on teaching.

In one sense the task for teachers will not change, since today we teach judgment more than facts, and the assessment of claims more than access to them. But we do not put these distinctions themselves in the foreground of our teaching. If the reason is that the competition with education from mere information has not yet called us to do so, then we should prepare to be called.

In short, nothing will change except that the temptations to resist will become nearly irresistible. There will be many more painless ways to teach badly, more excuses for those who want them, more dazzling distractions to the mission of liberating students from ignorance and cultivating their freedom to judge for themselves.

In Plato's *Meno*, Meno challenged Socrates with this dilemma. Why should we look for the truth? For if we know it already, then the search is superfluous; and if we don't know it already, then we wouldn't recognize it if we should ever find it. I'd like to revise Meno's dilemma for the information age. How can a titanic database serve undergraduate education? If we are already disciplinary experts, then it is too late; if we are not, then we are not ready for it yet and, until we are ready, it could do as much harm as good.

Socrates called Meno's dilemma a "trick argument"; I don't. The modern version applies, as I've indicated, just as much to libraries and textbooks as it does to databases. Students adrift in a large library know they need help, but not usually because they might run into interest-driven and methodologically-riven scholarship. But students adrift in a large database will probably not feel the same need for help. The small screen and game-like search commands prevent the sense of being lost; the aura of the computer deflects the fear of being duped. The risk of dupery is worrisome precisely for those students who don't worry about it.

Enhanced access to information is not hypothetical even if its extent and cost for any given near-future are unknown. It should cause teachers to reflect deeply on what they are trying to accomplish in the classroom. Teachers who know that their voice is only one among thousands or millions available to the student may try to use their position to color a student's judgment about the rest, but here progress is against them. We must educate students for intellectual autonomy, not discipleship, so they can navigate for themselves in the wilderness of information. Enhanced access to information will mean that we will be comic figures if we present our own views as if our critics were silent. We must present our considered views, of course, but for an audience that more and more will judge them in light of their alternatives. Our interest will not be to limit the alternatives students see but to make sure that students are able to make responsible judgments. This is not as easy as typing keywords at a terminal and catching a cascade of citations in a basket; it requires real teaching.

HOW TEACHERS TEACH, HOW STUDENTS LEARN: A HUMANIZING PROCESS

ALICE H. REICH

I want to begin with the briefest of deconstructions of myself, as Gayatri Spivak would say when you introduce yourself to an audience, you locate yourself. I am an anthropologist. I am much more a teacher than a researcher. I am much more a generalist than a specialist. When it comes to computers, I'm not cyberphobic, but I am skeptical. In fact, I can probably best locate myself with regard to a discussion about computers with the following epigram: "Where is the wisdom we have lost in knowledge, where is the knowledge we have lost in information?"

In order to address the role of computers in teaching, I had to ask myself once again those questions that we cannot ask ourselves too frequently. Who are our students? What is our discipline about, right now? What of that do we want to and can we convey in the classroom? What are our broader goals in teaching? Are they good goals? How can we best achieve them?

Thinking about all this in connection with computers adds an extra twist that makes it fun to think about all of this again. I'm going to try to say something first about teaching, then something about anthropology, next something about my students, and something about computers in relation to these things, and finally about the implications for pedagogy that I draw from these interconnections. No doubt it won't be quite that linear.

Reich is Professor of Sociology, Regis College, Denver, Colorado.

I begin from a belief that teaching is fundamentally a moral activity and that anthropology is fundamentally a moral discipline. I explored these ideas in a lecture delivered to my colleagues in 1982 where I argued that anthropology is the study of what it means to be human and teaching is the practice. Central to that argument is the definition of humans as, dialectically, the inheritors of and the creators of culture.

I would argue that the fundamental purpose of a liberal arts education is not skills training or knowledge acquisition, although those things should take place, but to humanize students and teachers alike. Humanizing is a process with no end. The purpose of a liberal arts education is to involve us all in the kinds of questions whose best answers are better questions, to create responsibility and hope in students and ourselves, and to empower students to the authentic use of language. I define that as the speaking that not only tells their stories but changes the world.

To be human, by my definition, is to recognize the right and necessity for all human beings to be makers of culture, as well as bearers of culture. You can see how that fits with education. We have both the right and the necessity to bear the knowledge of the past, but also to empower our students to create new knowledge. To be human is to have a voice that names the world in relation to one's own experience. To be human is to seize the right to one's own voice and to work for the rights of everyone to a voice.

When I say that teaching is a moral activity, I mean I intend the work I do to engage both myself and my students in the critical thought and action that will make this a better world. Our society appears to be suffering from a wide range and variety of ethical crises and of pain and disfunction in both public and private lives. I don't want to venture at this juncture an explanation of why this is so, but I'm moved by analyses such as those found in the book by Robert Bellah and his cohorts, *Habits of the Heart*, and by others who describe our problems as problems of individualism, nihilism, materialism, and greed.

I am *not* moved by the proposed solutions to those problems articulated by the "B Boys": Allan Bloom and William Bennett. They exhort us as educators to improve the situation through the inculcation of some eternal and absolute verities and values. I do care about developing a common language. I dream about it as Adrienne Rich does. I do care about public discourse and I regard teaching as a crucial place where we can take some first steps toward developing but not toward imposing such a language.

I'm interested in the analysis of our society in terms of nihilism. A man named Hubert Dreyfus at Berkeley has defined nihilism as the loss of intrinsic meaning, which he relates to a kind of social science. This social science is, according to Dreyfus, characterized by a kind of theorizing that objectifies and decontexturalizes in order to create comparability, predictability, and the like.

I think the computer is a perfect example of that kind of maker of meaninglessness, or that kind of loss of intrinsic meaning. The computer breaks down all symbols into equivalent bits. I do see computers as decontexturalizers, but I am open to education on that score.

I attempt to counter this nihilism in teaching with context, with human engagement, and with meaning; in this, I am very fortunate in my discipline. Cultural anthropology has as its subject matter meaningful human life in context. The exotic fact, the disgusting custom, the bits and pieces of cross cultural variety can be accumulated—talking about eating clotted blood is one way to wake students up at nine in the morning. This sort of thing can also make great cocktail party conversation, but it does not, in whatever numbers, add up to an understanding of the human experience.

To talk about human life as meaningful requires teaching that there are things that we cannot know, that there is mystery, that there are aspects of the lives of others that simply will never be open to us. Where students refuse to see the connections between their lives and lives of the Kung or the Dani or the poor of Reagan's America, for that matter, they have to be pushed to see the similarities. But likewise, when they attempt to reduce the complexities of other cultures into analogies with their own experiences they must be shown the unbridgeable gaps. I think that computers are not machines of mystery. They are mystifiers, which is a very different thing. Somebody once defined for me the difference between a mystery and a secret. A secret becomes less secret the more you know about it. A mystery becomes more mysterious the more you know about it.

The cultural relativism that is one of anthropology's greatest gifts is fundamental to a way of being in the world that can accept and celebrate human diversity, that can see diversity as a real human fact and asset, as a basis for communication and not for fear, domination, or ignoring. True communities are polyphonic. They have a lot of different voices. When you hear only one voice you're probably not in a community. I tend to see the computer as forcing uniformity, in spite of the obstacle of human variety, rather than celebrating diversity.

Another goal in trying to counter rampant forms of individualism is teaching that we are all connected, not only with others in our society, but with all humans who live and have lived. I think also it is crucial to try to empower students as makers of their world and makers of meaning in a contextualized social world.

I've thought a lot about the role of simulation in this kind of empowerment. If small children, for example, have a little universe in which they can do things and feel more powerful, that's great, but it has to be a step to getting out of that little universe into a bigger one. I send my students into real social settings to do their social observation. I am much happier to have them going into the hospital emergency room or a downtown mall in Denver than I am having them go into a lab and working with a simulated setting.

I understand the temptation to say "Couldn't I be a great teacher if only they gave me a better calibre of students?" The students I teach are not like I was. They're not even like most of the people with whom I went to college, and most of the people I went to college with didn't get Ph.D.s. They have experiences and needs and views of the world that are very distant to me. I never had the experience of being a mediocre student (which is not to say that I didn't flunk an Algebra test once in junior high, but I was *not* a mediocre student). I don't know what that feels like. A woman named Nel Noddings has written a book on education called *Caring*. She talks about when the student comes to you and says, "I have math anxiety." How tempting it is to try to entice that student into the beauty of math, rather than to try to understand what it feels like to be that student—which is really the more human response. These students come from different backgrounds, they've been socialized into a different society. They have different goals and they are going different places. I've had to do far more revising of my pedagogy in response to these differences than I think would ever be called for by any new technology.

I used to say with some glibness that while I was a follower of Paolo Freire and his pedagogy of the oppressed, I wasn't entirely sure how to translate it into a pedagogy of the oppressors, for I saw their relative financial privilege and white skins as a major defining feature of Regis College students. In fact, however, they do not as a rule trust their own voices any more than the Brazilian peasants with whom Freire worked.

Regis is not, in some ways, what is called a good college. I've been thinking a lot about that the last couple of days. One of the places I think computers may be empowering is in the equalizing function that people have talked about for these students. Most of my students do not come to me with a passion for learning. Most of my students come to get through the time. They want to get through the class, they want to get through college and then they are going to be in lives that they want to get through. That's disheartening, and we talk about that, but they do occasionally, often even, find that passion first in their attraction to ideas—particularly ideas that are different from those of their parents. In spite of my warning, they go home over spring break and try to argue, and they come back defeated. They want to learn then how to construct arguments. They want to learn how to win, and I think that access to the data is great. Perhaps a virtue of computers is in their ability to make those facts a little "cheaper"—a little more widely available—so that the empirical small arms are not sufficient to win and then a higher level of discussion can take place.

One of the first pedagogical changes I had to make was to do away with the term paper as it had been assigned throughout my undergraduate career. I'm interested to see the issue of plagiarism connected to technology, as it is in our conference materials, and technology may in fact make plagiarism easier. I'm not sure it will make it more common; I *am* sure that it's not the cause. When I began teaching I assigned research papers just as I had been assigned them in college—worth half the credit of the course, due at the end of the semester. I might ask for topics, but generally saw none of the work until I got the final papers. They often came as a great shock to me. I felt sad, I felt angry, I felt betrayed. They were either not the student's own work or not enough work, they used poor sources, there were bad research questions.

I moved intermediately to a multi-stage process in which I asked for topic and preliminary bibliography, then outline, then a narrative outline, then a first draft, then a final draft. This didn't work, at least not for most students, who would change topics, not hand in some of the stages, ignore my comments and advice, hand in something neither they nor I could care about. They never came in the next semester to pick up the paper, even though I'd written all those comments. So I now use, in place of that, something I call a research journal, and I'm far more pleased with the results. I ask them to do all the research that would be done and have it all documented. I do believe that research questions are much more important for my students than are the answers. I am more satisfied teaching the process of research than attending to the product. I do assign a variety of kinds of writing, and I use journals in different ways in different classes.

I also had to change pedagogy as I looked at what I and others call the hidden curriculum of my classroom. I wanted students to be active and responsible learners, yet I had learned to value and to produce tightly structured lectures, which gave me all the control and nearly the only voice in the classroom. Most of my classes now are conducted through discussion and I try to be quiet. If you sit quietly long enough, somebody will say something. How could I not be pleased if students had access to all kinds of information that I don't in that situation?

I believe that it is in relation to these students that I might have the most to learn about computers. They, the students, like them, I think, and I want to encourage that. They go to the library more because there are computers there. They will type papers on computers more readily than on typewriters. And I don't mind spell check at all (except for the way that it proofreads books!) I believe that the pedagogy that works best with the new technology is the pedagogy that works best without it—one that focuses on students, one that focuses on process.

How, now, can I say something about computers? I understand computers to be extremely rapid processors of a very small number of functions that are, in spite of the human analogy and life crisis language used around them, machines that are fundamentally different from humans. I don't see computers as intrinsically democratic or anti-democratic. I don't see them as intrinsically isolating or connecting, intrinsically empowering or alienating, intrinsically mystifying or demystifying. But I do care very much about how they are used with regard to these dichotomies.

My concerns with regard to computers are derived from my assumptions about what it means to be human. Hannah Arendt (in

The Human Condition) draws the distinction between a tool and a machine. The tool, she says, shapes itself to human rhythms while the machine shapes humans to its pace. It seems very important to me that we continue to ask the kinds of questions Roszak asks in *The Cult of Information* about, first of all, what are the *differences* between computer functioning and human minds, and, secondly, who is to be boss. A supermarket near my house installed machines that simulate voices and give the prices of items as they are scanned. The checkers move the items from the cart across the scanner, heads down. We refer to this place as the store where the machines talk to you and the people don't.

Something that is particularly dangerous in education is the emphasis on product. I again call on Hannah Arendt, who makes the distinction between work and action. Work is a process that proceeds from models towards specific goals and results in products, such as chairs. Action, on the other hand, is dialectical, dialogical, and open ended. It can occur only in human interaction and only in so far as the humans involved are truly human, that is, in my terms, they have a voice.

Action cannot be predicted, cannot be predictable, cannot have end products—cannot be oriented to ends, as a matter of fact. We have to have hope as we enter into action, we have to grieve the losses. It's a very powerful concept.

I think all of us as individuals and institutions are pressured to define education as an activity that results in some measurable product. I can give you a particularly horrendous example of this, unfortunately from my own institution, which increasingly uses the language of the marketplace. We sell or market education as an economically useful product to our consumers, and in some amazing transformation, our consumers become our products, which then go out on the market themselves. I suppose this is an issue for another forum, but I have seen the computer used much more easily and comfortably by those who see education as a product, or who see students as products. I regard that as a challenge to those of us of a different bent.

There are some very interesting things to think about in the relationship of computers to anthropology. Certainly on the ethnographic level, one can ask questions about how computers have changed the lives of people, how people think about and use computers, how we are affected by them, and what is happening in the work place with regard to health, privacy and civil rights.

I think there are equally interesting questions with regard to epistemology in anthropology. I think how ecstatic those nineteenth century guys would have been had they had computers. Their passion was the exhaustive listing and classifying of cultural traits and artifacts in the hope of bracketing human experience. Their goal was to be able to define what it was to be human by defining the varieties and the extremes of custom. This project was doomed to failure not just because, as those early anthropologists knew, whole societies were dying and being destroyed at such an awful rate, but because of the generativity, the creativity of human culture. As one of my graduate school professors would say, "If you can think of it, someone has done it, is doing it, or will be doing it soon."

Many anthropologists still have some of that nineteenth century natural history proclivity. I do. I am trying to create an exhaustive catalog of every named goddess, everywhere, from every culture in the world. How important it is for me that I have Reflex as a database to do this? When I began the project I used McBee punch cards.

There was another period in anthropology which I do believe and fervently hope has ended, during which quantitative approaches reigned. It was a kind of line-them-up-and-count-them notion of human behavior with an emphasis on measurement and prediction. At that time, interestingly enough, computers even for graduate students were pretty inaccessible. Now computers are everywhere. And we are into deconstruction—looking at lives and cultures as narrative constructions, analyzing them with the tools of rhetoric.

As to where I conclude, it's really fairly simple for me: in so far as the computer is empowering and humanizing students and the rest of us—I'm all for it. And since this will require my active involvement, this stance leaves me with both plenty of teaching and plenty of learning to do.

A GADFLY'S VIEW

DANIEL C. DENNETT

In his 1976 book, *The Selfish Gene*, Richard Dawkins defines a meme as a unit of culture that is subject to replication and selection. That is, memes are to cultural evolution what genes are to biological evolution. Examples of memes are such exalted cultural objects as theories of plate tectonics, or Newtonian physics, or Einsteinian relativity theory, symphonies, theological principles, or such lowly objects as advertising jingles, food fads, slang terms, and computer programs. Technological innovations are memes and so are behavioral or organizational innovations. Television is a meme. Another is the use of television in the classroom. The idea of the computer is a meme and so is the idea of using a computer in the classroom. Memes have physical embodiments—printed in books, painted on walls, molded into vinyl disks, magnetically preserved on floppy disks, stored in libraries, and more.

Their replication and preservation depends on human brain activity. Some have vivid but brief periods of popularity followed by near extinction, such as "Where's the beef?" hoola hoops, canasta, stereopticon pictures, and other technological turkeys of the past and future. Others seem to be with us for the long run—long division, Christianity, newspapers, television.

I propose that we follow Richard Dawkins and adopt the meme's eye view. A motto for this—which I like because it nicely

Dennett is Director, Center for Cognitive Studies, and Co-Director, Curricular Software Studio, Tufts University, Medford, Massachusetts.

plays on an old evolutionary theme that a chicken is just an egg's way of making another egg—is "A scholar is just a library's way of making another library."

I agree with the idea that technological determinism is wrong and I want to help to explain why it is so hard to predict the technological future and control it. We may be grateful that it's hard to predict, but we may *not* be so grateful that it's hard to control. The reason that it is hard to predict and control the technological future is the same reason that it's hard to predict and control evolutionary future—the evolutionary process is a noise amplifier and, in general, an extremely devious and complicated process.

I want to make clear from the outset that I do not view Dawkins' claims about memes to be a metaphor. I view this to be a literal truth and I might say, so does Dawkins. He argues with great eloquence and persuasiveness that evolutionary theory applies literally and exactly to cultural evolution, if you understand it correctly and if you establish the right units of replication—which he takes to be memes.

The most important thing to understand about memes is that they are, as Dawkins says, selfish—selfish in the same sense that genes are selfish. The reproductive success of the meme is largely independent of its value to us. When people talk about the "survival of the fittest" they usually have in mind by "the fittest" those ideas, cultural innovations, and technological innovations that are best suited for us. But that is *not* how the selfish meme is defined. "The fittest" are those that replicate best, independently of whether or not they are good for us. Quite independent of their value to us (their creators), "the fittest" are the ones that reproduce. This principle—that the reproductive success of a meme is largely independent of us—has set the problem before us now. The problem is to diminish that independence, to increase our control over what we might call the infosphere (analogous to the biosphere). The infosphere is the gene pool of memes, the "meme pool" if you like.

This idea of the infosphere may be new, but the phenomenon is not. Before Gutenburg, in the days of writing on papyrus, for example, there was memic replication, reproduction, and transmission. The only thing that has changed is that we have new media now—new cultures in the biological sense—in which memes can replicate and reproduce. This has changed the physics of meme reproduction—and use and mutation—in some rather striking ways, and is what creates the current crisis.

Memes are (in Dawkins' conceptualization) trying to replicate, and they succeed very well if they end up in large numbers in data banks and libraries. If you record a "platinum" record, a "hit," there will be many, many copies of that particular meme spread all over the world. But how many of us today can recognize *all* the Top Ten songs of, say, 1955? If a tune not only runs through everybody's head, but moreover is passed on to children and grandchildren, then that's a meme that is going to survive for several human generations in multiple copies in multiple individuals. Most memes, however, end up in the dump.

Human beings are the primary vehicles of memes, and we should recognize that these carriers of memes have boundaries around them—we all have filters. There are too many memes out there, and no one of us carries all of them, or wants to carry all of them, or can carry all of them. So we have filters around ourselves to protect us from overload of various sorts, so that each one of us only carries a certain subset of the memes that are available in the infosphere at any one time. This is a very powerful organizing principle.

To give an example I will tell a story. A friend of mine, John McCarthy, is one of the pioneers of artificial intelligence. He invented the term "artificial intelligence," which is one of the most well replicated memes around. About ten years ago while at Stanford at the Center for Advanced Study in Behavioral Sciences John, myself, and several other people were working on artificial intelligence and philosophy. This was at the very dawn of the microcomputer era—I saw my first Apple that year. It was not out of the garage yet.

In a talk at the center, John was trying to persuade people of the glories of what we now know as electronic mail, or e-mail. John gave a visionary talk about how this brand new medium was going to transform the world for everyone. Throwing some sops to the humanists, he said, "Think about poetry. It's very hard for a poet to make a living today, because if you're a poet and you want to be a published poet, the only chance you ever have is if you get your poems into a 'slender volume.' There are only a few publishers who publish them and they are terribly expensive. Most poets don't get published and if you never make it into these slender volumes, that's it, you can never make a dime as a poet."

He continued, "When we have this vast informational network, the electronic network, where everybody is all hooked up, poets will be able to do this: They will be able to put their poems online, and, for a penny, anybody can read their poems. Since these poems will be broadcast all over the world, the poets' bank accounts will electronically accrue sums of money, a modest living or a fortune, depending on how many customers will spend an electronic penny." Well, it was a nice idea but what John had failed to realize (and obviously hadn't thought about very much), was that there are very good reasons for those slender volumes.

Face the fact: if you are on electronic mail and you see when you log on in the morning that 350,000 poets would like to sell you a poem, what are you going to do? If you're interested in poetry, you will want to subscribe to a service that filters those poems down through an elaborate editorial process. But first you'll subscribe to another service that tells you which of the 157 available poetry filtering services are good for the sort of poetry you like. Eventually, you'll end up reading just a carefully hand-selected group of poems. This will be a slender electronic volume, which will cost just about as much as today's hard-bound book. There will be just as few poets who actually make a living at poetry.

You don't solve the problem by simply changing the medium. An interesting footnote to this story is that John McCarthy, who trumpeted the virtues of electronic mail in those days, has now decided that electronic mail is a future turkey; it's on its way out. He believes it will be replaced by fax, for the very simple reason that for all of the virtues of e-mail over fax, communicating with people by e-mail is user-unfriendly because it's so hard to address them. With the telephone, and hence fax, all you have to know is somebody's telephone number, whereas with e-mail, two computers can't talk to each other unless they have been properly introduced. It reminds me of what Britain used to be like—two people couldn't talk to each other unless they had been properly introduced, even if they were standing right next to each other.

What John McCarthy's example nicely illustrates is the importance of the filters with which we surround ourselves. Consider a few of the other implications of this competition between memes. It's not enough simply to publish a book. You must get your book reviewed. It's not enough that you get your book reviewed; it has to be reviewed in the right places. It's not enough that you get your book reviewed in the right places. The right people have to notice that your book got reviewed in the right places. Now if you can get your book on the list of books that have been well reviewed, and can get that list onto somebody's list of lists of books that have been well reviewed, then pretty soon your book is actually going to have some impact. It's actually going to spread its memes through the infosphere, and if it fails to do that, then, as Hume said several centuries ago, "It falls dead born from the press."

Publishers talk of lift-off. They now invest huge sums of money in advertising books hoping to get them on the best seller lists. If they can for just one week, one minute, get their book on the best seller list, then a sort of recursive process takes over. People notice the book because other people have been noticing the book. Lift-off occurs and then all the money they have been putting into advertising pays for itself many times over as the book spreads rapidly through the infosphere. That is how best sellers are made. (This point is made by Richard Dawkins in *The Blind Watchmaker*.)

Notice that the same thing happens with much smaller amounts of money at stake or when money is not the issue at all—for example, in the academic world. Think about your own field, about how there are articles or books that achieve fame or notoriety, are regularly assigned in class, are anthologized over and over again, not so much for their intrinsic scholarly merit but, for instance, because they beautifully express a simple-minded version of a view that you would like to present in class in a way that is accessible enough so that the students can get the thrill of refuting a published article.

Wherever you have evolution and evolutionary niches you get one niche begetting another niche by creating opportunities for parasites—that is to say meretricious memes insinuating themselves in various ways. This is most obvious fashion when we look at the highways springing up in every roughly urban area and even in many rural areas. It's known as the commercial strip, where all the McDonalds, car dealerships, and other establishments line up, put up giant signs, and then put up bigger and bigger signs to attract the attention of the passing motorist. This phenomenon of runaway advertising is a clear analog of biological phenomena such as what

R.A. Fisher called "runaway sexual selection," which helps to explain the peacock's tail and other luxuries of nature.

We see the same thing in our own academic spheres where we have severe competition for memes, abetted and aided in many regards by what can only be called advertising. The problem for any meme, or any lover of a particular meme (and we all love our own memes) is how to catch the attention of our target audience when its attention is being attracted by literally thousands or millions of competitors.

Another example of the effects of meme competition is the role of the new media in changing the parameters of that meme competition. A library has a filter around it; it doesn't buy everything in print. I once concocted what I thought was a rather clever line about libraries: A good library is a library with all the good books in it and a great library is a library with all the books in it. The difference between them is that a good library doesn't have all the second-rate books that a great library also has.

This situation, however, is rapidly changing to the point where any library can be a great library. Any library is going to be able to have, with negligible amounts of time and inconvenience, just about anything anyone wants. Back when my slogan looked like a good slogan, the individual library user was more or less on his or her own to know how to use that resource, but that's what great libraries were for. They put a certain demand on the individual to be able to find his or her way through that vast supply. Soon we will be faced with a paradoxical situation: What are we going to do when *all* our libraries are great libraries? When the boundary around the library no longer makes much of a difference, the individual using that library becomes much more of a problem.

Suppose my vision of the infosphere and this competition of memes is not just a metaphor, but is taken literally. If meme evolution is an exact and literal analog of gene evolution, various sorts of opportunities should be created for arms races, viruses, counter viruses, parasites, counter parasites and the like. Here are a few examples. The computer virus is a particularly graphic, concrete version of a runaway meme inhabiting the current physical structures of the infosphere. Here is another meme parasiting a technological innovation: a fundamentalist religious group installed an 800-number telephone line with religious messages. Someone who disapproved of this religious group wrote a clever little computer program that would call up this number thousands of times a day. Since it was an 800-number the charges were made to the religious group. The program succeeded in running up a bill in just a few days of well over a million dollars. This exploited one meme with another meme in a rather dramatic way.

Then there is the counter-meme operating in the niche created by science citation indexes: The practice, now spreading through certain scientific areas, of authors deliberately misspelling the names of authors they cite in their articles, so those other authors will not get credit in the citation index. The computer program, which notes frequency of citations, is not flexible and does not notice misspellings—thus guaranteeing that at least this article will not contribute to another author's citation index quotient. One can immediately imagine the counter-memes—minor alterations of the computer program, making it slightly more flexible and able to look for spelling variances. We are now off on an arms race. Imagine the counter-moves to that.

These new technologies have simply radicalized the process in the infosphere by changing the physics of it—not physics in the obvious way—just using electronics as opposed to using paper and pencil, although that is the heart of it. I'm thinking, rather, about properties that have been very important in the infosphere until now—inertia, for example. Peter Suber has talked about the importance of a hardcover book that one can hold, that has a certain concrete reality. For several centuries that particular embodiment of memes has been taken for granted. It created a certain important inertia in the infosphere, which is very important and which is now beginning to erode.

For instance, we now have a problem of citation. Very often I first come across an article in an electronic version sent to me by e-mail. I may get a hard-copy version of the second draft a little bit later, circulating as a pre-print or draft. Sometime after that, maybe two or three years later, it is finally published, drastically revised, in some journal.

Which version of it do I cite? I may have been citing it in pre-print form for several years. What is considered the definitive edition of anything now that we have electronic media, which is subject to redrafting with such tremendous ease? We have all noticed this phenomenon—a certain loss of definition of what counts as the canonical text of anything—whether it's lecture notes, a letter, or any other isolated hunk of text. What we've lost is, in effect, the inertia provided by the physical media, which until very recently more-or-less guaranteed the identity of a particular textural embodiment of a meme.

This raises problems of the following sort. I receive pre-prints, both electronically and through the mail. What has happened is that there is now—no doubt in almost every field, certainly in mine at the research levels—an informal grapevine of people who are on each others' pre-print list, either electronically or by mail. Now, consider the brightest person in the world, a young scholar in some area of cognitive science who, after receiving his or her Ph.D., goes off to teach somewhere and somehow or other doesn't get on the preferred pre-print list. That person can religiously go to the library and read the journals the day they come out—but that person will be already two or three years behind. Unless that person is on the favored elite grapevine of pre-print circulations, he or she might just as well be sitting on a desert island getting journals by a slow boat.

Now I want to pose a problem using the idea of the memosphere. Each one of us is surrounded by a tremendous barrage of memes and our set of filters to deal with the tremendous amount of information surrounding us. We have to decide: Which network news are we going to listen to (if we listen to any network news)? Are we going to trust the *New York Times*, get several radical newspapers, or settle for *McNeil-Lehrer*? Which journals are we going to read? Which reviews are we going to read?

The trouble is, no filter is or could be foolproof. The whole point of a filter is that it is, to some degree, arbitrary. It takes a large mass of information on whatever topic and does some sort of a "kiss and a promise" diminution of that information. What do I mean by foolproof? An individual's filters would be foolproof if the only memes that finally get through were exactly the memes that ought to get through—the ones that are of most use, the best, those that provide the clearest vision, the best chance of doing whatever that person's projects are in the world, and of guiding that person's actions in the best way.

We are all faced with this problem and we all have to erect filters. Some of these filters are, by the way, metafilters. They provide advice about which filters to use and how to use them. Some of these are people—professors, advisors and friends.

But no filter is foolproof. It follows that there could not be a technological solution to the filtering problem. All one can do is choose one set of technological filters or another. There is no escape from the dependence on those filters (which are never foolproof) so there cannot be a technological solution to the problem. But your closest advisors—your professors, your friends—are just as biased, just as susceptible to misperception, misunderstanding, and a biased filtering of information as any technological device could be, so we have a serious problem.

That there cannot be a human solution as well as a technological solution seems to have very important ethical implications. I discussed these in two articles. The first, "Information, Technology and the Virtues of Ignorance" (Daedalus [Summer 1986]: 135-53) concerns itself with the varieties of virtue which are available only if you are ignorant—and excusably ignorant—and the problems that arise when, thanks to technology, we no longer have the excuse of ignorance.

The second, "The Moral First Aid Manual," appears in *The Tanner Lectures* (Ann Arbor, 7 November 1986). The titles of these two pieces give some sense of the urgency I consider this moral problem to have. While I've already said there can't be an optimal technological or human solution—we *can* talk about partial solutions.

What we want to do is make the individual as powerful as possible, relative to the memes and the filters. The filters themselves are just more memes. It's all memes out there. Some of them are meta-memes—filters on other memes. The most we can do is enhance the power of the individual, increase the power of the functional anatomy of the individual to deal with and make wise choices regarding the management of this meme invasion.

Biology Professor Jerry Woolpy attempts to teach his students the structure of the infosphere and raise their consciousness about the filters on it. That is a meta-meme of which I heartily endorse replication.

The only way to fight memes is with more memes, that is, harness the technology itself to enhance the individual. In 1982, in a piece called "Notes on Prosthetic Imagination" (*Boston Review* [June 1982]: 3-7), I discussed how computers, in principle, could be used to expand the powers of imagination. As luck would have it (luck enters into these things very often; that's why it's so hard to predict), the editor of that issue of the *Boston Review* was Eric Wanner, who went on from there to be a program officer at the Sloan Foundation. He decided to put some of that foundation's money where my mouth was. He said, "You think you can enhance the power of individuals with some of these technologies, so why don't you try to do it?"

I thought I was just being a philosopher, talking about what it would be nice to do. The next thing I knew, I was given some money so I could actually do it. The Curricular Software Studio was set up at Tufts University. The name was chosen with some care. It is not a lab and it is not a workshop. It's a studio, because what we do there is as much art as technology. It's a studio in the Renaissance sense. It has patrons—professors with projects. The professors come to the studio with a pedagogical problem, a bottleneck—something they are finding difficult to convey to their students. They have a vague sense of how we might use a computer to open up this bottleneck, to enhance the powers of their students to understand some complex materials. We put such a patron in touch with our artists, who are fine hackers, professional computer programmers. My role is to play matchmaker and midwife, bringing together these two parties and helping them design a new meme-machine, a tool that will expand the imagination and conceptual powers of individual students.

Here are two different ways in which tools can enhance human powers. One way might be called the "bulldozer" way, where a relatively puny 98-pound weakling can sit and push buttons and make great things happen. Automobiles, bulldozers, and cranes are that sort of power magnifier. So are large databases. In general, computers magnify our powers in the bulldozer sense.

Contrast that kind of power amplification with a different kind, which has only recently become popular: the Nautilus machine, which uses technology to increase the actual individual human strength of the person who exercises with it.

These are both technology, but with very different aspirations. The bulldozer doesn't make you, personally, stronger, but if you want to move heavy things, it's a great tool. You can become dependent on it, in fact. The Nautilus machine, on the other hand, can enable you to walk away from it and lift heavy weights. That's a different sort of amplification of power. It is power that comes back to you, so when you walk away from the technology you actually have more power than when you started—you take it with you. In the software studio, we are devising Nautilus machines for the mind.

One of the first projects we undertook was an introductory course in computer science itself. In this large class of relatively computer-phobic students, the single greatest impediment to their learning anything was fear—not just fear of the computer, but fear of problem solving, of the very idea of getting into a problem-solving mentality. These were not the sort of student who liked to solve crossword puzzles or play word games. These were students who, if given a choice between doing a crossword puzzle and memorizing the telephone book, would rather memorize the telephone book.

What can you do when this is the problem with which you are starting? You begin by creating tiny problem spaces where the choices are so small that even the most terrified problem solver, by brute force elimination of the alternatives, will be able to solve tiny problems. We invented a little computer (a register machine) called RODREGO where there are only two operations from which to choose—increment a register or decrement a register—and, in no time, we had our students writing quite elaborate little routines for this register machine, "teaching" it to do arithmetic, to copy contents, to test conditions, and so forth. We went on to fancier machines. We moved a group of students who were terrified of thinking (as opposed to memorizing) and seduced them. We showed them that they could succeed in thinking through problems and building on their successes.

The machines we build are not teachers. They are not designed to replace teachers or tutors. They are something different. If anything, they are vehicles for exploring certain spaces. They permit the individual to get into them and drive them around through mental spaces that have complex properties. In the process of essentially free exploration of those terrains, the individual gains knowledge and understanding.

For example, we have a machine in anesthesiology created for medical students. It's rather like a flight simulator, teaching one how to "fly" in the operating room as an anesthesiologist. It starts with a picture of the animal in question. It shows the lungs, the tanks of anesthetic, the blood pressure, the skeleton, and the relationship between skeletal weight and muscle weight. It also shows an array of dials, which register the important features of the patient through the operation. Once you get really good at "flying" the patient, you can turn to "instrument flying." The pictures disappear once you've internalized the model. Then you're on your own with just the dials and gauges and you've got to keep the patient alive. That's the way anesthesiologists actually operate under current circumstances. They must do instrument flying. This software provides a model they can internalize so that once they have it vividly in their heads, they can do instrument flying, because they know what all these dial readings really mean.

These are the vehicles we are building. They are not question-answering systems. They are not CAI. They are not appropriate for all disciplines. In fact, in the four years or so that I have been running the studio, I haven't been able to think of a single good application of the studio's vision to philosophy, my own discipline.

There are other systems the studio would love to build, because they are both harder in a certain way and more exciting than the ones we've already built. To date the ones that have had the most success have been in the sciences—population genetics, computer science, neuroanatomy, statistics, geology, anesthesiology. But one of my favorite ideas has been what I call the Latin Grammar Hyper-Cube. The idea for this came from helping my son with his Latin. It brought back unhappy memories of learning Latin when I was a high school student.

The traditional grammarians knew enough to use lots of mneumonic cues. For instance, in the upper left hand corner, was always first person singular; third person plural was in the lower right hand corner. This spatial arrangement remains constant through all arrays of grammatical types—singular to the left, plural to the right, and so forth. Realizing that the traditional Latin grammars were actually wonderfully constructed multidimensional spaces, it occurred to me that without doing any violence to the traditional categories, one could recast all of that into what might be called a hyper cube, which could be displayed graphically in a computer. It would consist of a cube that lines up the conjugations and declensions of Latin in different planes and color codes them. Fonts could be used to code something—perhaps masculine, feminine, and neuter. Upper case/lower case could code something else. This would create a logical space that one could go zooming around as if in a spaceship. You could go zinging down the ablative absolute looking at the variations encountered along the way. This program would be great fun to write, especially fiddling with all the variations and dimensions to discover the pedagogically nicest version.

There are two other language systems I'd like to see done. One evolved during a vacation in Mexico where I became interested in Mayan hieroglyphics, which though forbiddingly difficult, are quite beautiful and interesting. Many people get interested in Mayan hieroglyphics, but very few ever learn how to read them.

Almost all Mayan hieroglyphics have to do with calendar dates, and the Mayan calendrical systems don't line up with ours. That is, they line up beautifully but not always in phase. First, then, imagine a time line system showing where the corrections are made in the various juxtaposed calendar systems. Then any date can be re-presented both as a mark on the juxtaposed time lines, and as a Mayan glyph. Imagine having something like the odometer of a car that you can spin to different dates, and watching the hieroglyphics change as you change the dates. You could watch the periodicities that were in common with the time lines and the changing forms in the hieroglyphics. A program could be developed to teach even not very interested freshmen how to read Mayan hieroglyphics, an advanced and subtle competence that many archeology students never get around to learning.

This illustrates a problem we keep coming up against: professors who, for very good reasons, are victims and perpetrators of a self-fulfilling prophecy. They simply decide that there is something too difficult for their students—at least too hard using the techniques they have had up until now. They are loathe to try to teach their students something that has been accessible only to a tiny fraction up until now. Most people who teach courses in Mayan archeology at the undergraduate level are not going to bother trying to teach their students to read hieroglyphics. I submit that there is no reason not to aspire to that.

One more language example, one that employs a different use of a technology that has been quite properly maligned by many commentators: interactive videodisks. I have not been a fan of interactive videodisks. I dragged my feet for two or three years because most of the applications I had seen were boring—offensively boring sometimes. I was not inclined to think there was anything very interesting to do with interactive videodisks until this project came along. It's in French.

What happens in foreign language instruction, as in just about any field, is that it begins by over-simplifying, idealizing, and tidying up the subject so that it's initially accessible to students. That's pedagogical wisdom. Students in French class learn a language, sort of French, but it is the peculiar idealized French learned in French I, II, III, and IV, and is really nobody's natural language. It's an idealized, oversimplified, ersatz French, which allows one to read French newspapers and books, and even follow French films and some French television. But, when the students then encounter the French of people on the street, or in a free-for-all discussion, they get swamped by complications they have been spared until then. They get lost in conversational French, simply because real honest-to-goodness, unscripted, uncleaned-up French occupies a rather different place in a rather more complicated space than the French they are taught.

Traditional pedagogy says one should teach the students the ersatz, idealized French and then send them out to learn all of the curlicues, or some of the curlicues, on their own. They learn some of the messiness on their own in the hustle and bustle of casual interaction with French people.

We can do better than that. Working with Lawrence Wiley at Harvard and a few other people, we have created videotaped, candid, unscripted, native French conversations. The frames are all numbered and ordered and are now getting packed on the videodisk. The advantage of using videodisks is they can be slowed, stopped, sped up, run backwards, changed in speed, sound dropped out, and sounds brought in. Segments can be distilled and analyzed any way you like at the push of a button. It is hoped that this will enable us to take the casual and chaotic experience that a French IV graduate gets living in France and compress it, distill it, make it more efficient, drawing attention to the ways in which French people can interrupt each other, the ways in which gesture, intonation, and position matter. The idea is not to turn students into people who can pass for true Parisians (although that might be one of the aspirations of it), but simply to enhance their passage through this bottleneck.

In his book *Mindstorms*, Seymour Papert talks about what he calls the Qwerty phenomenon—the settling for the suboptimal solution because of the vagaries of history. It's the problem of the standard Qwerty typewriter. Once a system of typewriting becomes established, it's extremely hard to dislodge even though there are other typewriter keyboards that are demonstratively better. The costs of getting from one to the other are so great that the chances at going for a better solution are lost.

How does one get there from here? Evolutionary theory has the lovely idea of an adaptive landscape. An adaptive landscape is an abstract three-dimensional landscape where one can plot out various features. The high places—the hilltops—are the good places. Evolutionary theory tells us that organisms tend to cluster in the good places. The question is, how to get organisms across a valley to another envisaged good place that might be higher, closer to a global maximum rather than a local maximum, but that involves descending into a valley to get there.

As well as an interesting problem in evolutionary theory, this is also a problem in the evolution of memes. Suppose we were all sitting atop the local suboptimal hilltop of television and we wanted to get to another hilltop—the hilltop of the VCR. As explained by Martin Dillon, the only way to get there was by a bridge—the pornography bridge. How the state of the world changed, from everybody owning television sets to everybody owning VCRs, according to Dillon, was that people wanted to buy pornographic home videos. They provided the market infrastructure so that VCRs could then become established and then everybody had to have one, whether or not they wanted to watch pornography at home.

A bridge is necessary in order to get across to an envisioned high point. We see much the same thing going on right now. Everyone uses word processing. The bridge has been crossed and there is no going back. Aren't there some hills in the distance in word processing that we can see and would like to get to? Can we build bridges to them? The answer is not at all clear, because the economic problems—the valleys—are very severe.

The systems we're building at the Software Studio cost between a quarter million and a half million dollars each. It's very expensive, taking 2,000 to 5,000 hours of expert time to create a single product, plus thousands of hours of student programming. If a product is created that is largely inexhaustible in its use, as an exploration vehicle tends to be, many, many hours can be spent using it. That's one of its virtues. But the initial investments are very large.

There are other problems as well. One of them is that most of our students aren't like us. They are not professors and aren't going to be. They are not turned on by the things that turn us on. Those of us doing the software have our own aesthetics, which determines the things we really admire, the things that excite us. Most of our students don't share our attitudes or aesthetics at all. We fear we are passing up exploration vehicles that would be much more effective than the ones we are actually doing. For instance, I recently explored a highly touted educational simulation running on a Mac. I hated it. I felt offended, insulted, manipulated. I thought it was cheap. Then I discovered that, because my reactions were so negative, I wasn't even interested in finding out whether the students using it were actually learning the material. For all I know, it works wonders for the students it was designed to serve. I'd hate to believe it, but it might be true. I submit that it is a serious problem when professors try to impose their own aesthetics on what they are doing—sometimes at the cost of their students, but I don't know how to avoid it.

When you take the meme's eye point of view you notice a serious problem—the problem of filtering. There is no definitive solution. There is no such thing as a foolproof filter. The closest solution we can have is to find ways to empower the individual more. The only way you can really empower individuals in dealing with memes is with more memes. You can teach these memes to them by talking, or you can give them technological memes. But they're all just memes. We must try to find the right memes to give our students to empower them to deal with other memes.

Our best hope is to befriend the best meta-memes we can find, and then do our best to replicate them in our colleagues and students. I hope my memes have gotten through your filters and you find them worth using and replicating in others. **

** Since this presentation was given at Earlham College I have published a more systematic discussion of memes, in "Memes and the Exploitation of Imagination," *Journal of Aesthetics and Art Critism.* I have also given up the co-directorship of the Tufts Curricular Software Studio, which continues to work on the projects described here under the able direction of George Smith, and with my continued informal support.

SILICON BASEMENTS AND THE LIBERAL ARTS: ONE DEAN'S PERSPECTIVE

DIANE BALESTRI

Let's imagine together that you are the faculty and I am an academic dean at a fine, small liberal arts college not unlike Earlham College, where we have the pleasure of sitting this morning. As dean of this small college, I am aware of the rapid proliferation of shiny little computer screens across our campus. My secretary has one, of course. But it's the presence of computers in the academic buildings that has captured my attention. In the physics laboratory, students are using computers as instruments to collect data and analyze it; then they use the same computers to graph their data and to generate lab reports. My colleagues in the English Department, most of whom have their own word processors, are rethinking their writing assignments based on the assumption that students can revise their drafts more easily in our basement computer clusters. When I use the library catalog, I find myself logging on rather than flipping through long rows of cards. And now the librarian at a neighboring institution is holding this conference to explore the assumption that technology will soon be able to provide my faculty members and their students with "unlimited information access."

The image of my hitherto orderly institution being over-whelmed with an undifferentiated tidal wave of "information" is at

Balestri is Assistant Dean of the College, Princeton University, Princeton, New Jersey.

first alarming. How will teaching and learning be affected by this new environment? Will students be smothered, bewildered, perplexed? Or, in self-defense, will they become impervious, simply indifferent to an endless array of information they cannot understand? How will they learn to sort out significant information from the mass of distracting irrelevancy? Or will they enclose themselves in the small shell of the close-at-hand, the familiar, the superficial? Will the humanistic and liberal learning that we value be lost?

Our students' twenty-first-century world of work and even of leisure will require them to manage just such vast quantities of information, I know. I realize that our institution, like all institutions of higher learning, must help our students learn to understand how to live in an environment overflowing with information. Turning our backs on this future is not possible. Instead we must decide how information technology can be brought into the classroom, how the ivory tower can make the best use of its silicon basements,[1] in order to prepare students responsibly for the world they will inhabit. So, this morning, with you, my faculty colleagues, I will try to take that overwhelming image—the tidal wave of information—and make it a catalyst for re-examining some of our institution's basic assumptions about how and what students can and should be learning.

As dean and faculty, we together define the scope of the learning that goes on at our college. We set goals for our students—what we want them to learn. We embody those goals in a particular set of curricular requirements or curricular opportunities—how we want students to learn. Finally, we work with our colleagues in the academic departments and in other college offices to create the teaching and learning environment that enables our students to achieve these goals. Let me review our current position on these matters.

First, the goals. As faculty members across the disciplines, we have concrete goals for our students. We want them to be active and independent learners. We also want our students to achieve a degree of mastery. By "mastery" we mean some specific expertise—a set of skills, knowledge of a corpus of material, familiarity with a disciplinary discourse. By "mastery" we also mean a general intellectual maturity, flexibility with a broad range of materials, and judgment to distinguish what's important from what's not. We actually extend these goals even further: our students should be able not only to master skills or bodies of knowledge but also to construct new knowledge for themselves.

Second, the curriculum. We try to embody these goals in the way we structure our students' learning. To promote active learning, we require students to tackle a variety of different subjects; we ask them to conduct experiments, to write, to converse. To help them achieve a sense of mastery, we require students to choose a discipline, learn its methodology, and study its content. Finally we assign open-ended experiments, independent projects, and senior theses to give students the opportunity to generate new knowledge.

Third, the learning environment. When I look around at the classrooms, laboratories, libraries, and even the residential areas of our institution, I see that we already have in place a complex, heterogeneous set of facilities, which are attractive and quite successful as an environment for learning. I see an excellent faculty, and other staff members—librarians, technicians, laboratory coordinators, to name only a few—who support the institution's teaching mission. In the laboratories, libraries, and even in a little museum, I see many material resources that support various kinds of active learning. I see a body of good students who are great learning resources for one another; an admissions staff that helps determine the quality and diversity of that student body; and a set of residential halls and residential services for them. All these resources are valuable and expensive. They serve the academic mission of our institution well. Not one is likely to diminish as a recurring expense in the college's budget.

In the context of our goal to create and sustain a community of active learners, and given the many resources already in place to meet that goal, why should I—as an academic dean—speak up for yet another expensive resource for our students? Where does information technology fit into this picture? Is it a threat to our values or an asset? Should I encourage or discourage its expansion?

Unlike some others, I see the potential impact of information technology on our institution as neither negligible nor negative. We should not fear that computers are spigots, that when opened will simply drown our students in a wash of irrelevant data. Computers are indeed powerful tools that create new access to much information, to many resources for learning in every discipline. But computers are simultaneously powerful tools for managing these resources, for turning abundant information to the purposes of new and more effective learning. In deciding how to use both the resources and the tools of information technology on our campus, we should look at some of the ways in which computers on other campuses are helping to promote active learning, mastery of content and process in various disciplines, and independent thinking—the same goals that we have already set for students' learning.

We will most commonly discover the computer functioning as a tool for acquiring and managing large quantities of information at the most advanced stages of learning, particularly in independent research. At the library, computers connect students to local catalogs and distant databases; they help students identify, sort, store, and organize bibliographic information. In a similar way, students in molecular biology log on to networks to gather and analyze information from enormous national databases of gene sequences as an integral and increasingly routine part of their research.

Much earlier in students' careers, in their earliest classroom or homework assignments, faculty members on many campuses promote active learning by introducing this same research strategy: opening access to relevant bodies of information while giving students useful tools for exploring those materials, "handling" the information in various ways, storing selections from it, and incorporating it into their written work. George Landow at Brown University provides his students of nineteenth century English literature with a rich electronic database of cultural, historical, and social resources (including text, pictures, and time lines). He invites them to explore that database, also called a "hypertext," by following "links" or connections that he and previous students have established, or by creating links of their own. Landow's purpose is to teach students how to negotiate a mass of material in order to develop a coherent and personally meaningful context for the literature they are reading. Similarly, Greg Crane at Harvard University uses compact disk technology in his Perseus project to provide students with a large store of visual images as well as texts for the study of classical Greece. Here, as in Landow's project, both the process and content of learning in an information-rich environment can be guided by a teacher's links or can be explored freely by the student.

These examples demonstrate how students can learn to control a broad spectrum of information. Information, and the process of gaining understanding from it, can also be presented to students in innovative formats that teach them how to query a body of information for study in depth. Carnegie Mellon Professor David Miller's Great American History Machine allows students to select their own sets of United States census data, display their numerical data graphically on county or state maps, and literally see and compare the resulting demographic patterns. Preston Covey and Scott Roberts, also at Carnegie Mellon University, took the footage from a documentary film and turned it into an award-winning case study, stored on an interactive videodisk, that encourages students to explore the difficult moral issues surrounding Dax Cowart's physical suffering from terrible burns and his request that he be allowed to die.

In all four of these examples, the computer opens a particular world of information to students and helps them to see, study, and draw conclusions from the data, and ultimately to create for themselves meaningful patterns from the information. Faculty members are also introducing computers in the classroom as tools that enable students to practice the skills of various disciplines, and from "learning by doing" to develop mastery. Used this way, the computer becomes exactly the kind of robust "Nautilus machine" for the mind that Daniel Dennett mentions elsewhere in this book. Here are two examples.

My first examples of computer-based "Nautilus machines" introduce students to the practice of revision, the art of "doing it again thoughtfully." Students can use their computers as convenient and helpful tools for practicing the cycle of active learning: brainstorming or experimenting, organizing materials, drafting solutions, receiving critiques, revising, and experimenting or drafting some more. This strategy is obviously facilitated in writing courses by simple word processing. But a simulated genetics laboratory, like the Genetics Toolkit developed by John Jungck at Beloit College, can provide students with a similar opportunity: using the Toolkit, they can plan an experimental strategy, try it out quickly across many "generations" of simulated fruit flies, evaluate the results, refine the experiment, carry out further testing, and present conclusions.

The second sort of computer-based "Nautilus machine" is a communication system that develops good habits of sharing information. Students learn how to collaborate in collecting and evaluating information and in presenting the results of their work. Earlier in this publication, our colleague Fred Goodman described a wonderful environment for collaboration among a group of students studying global politics. Goodman's computers create a network for communication among the collaborating students, who represent the viewpoints of different nations; the network also offers a common workspace in which information from these different sources can be shared, collated, and reconfigured by the whole group as they develop a model simulation for high school students.

Finally, we can look at some ways in which computers support our third and final goal: that students become creators of new works and of new knowledge. The computer is an important professional tool for composing, for designing new objects or works of art across all the disciplines in which creativity is traditionally encouraged: music, architecture, computer programming, graphic arts, writing. Students at many institutions already benefit from learning to use such tools as computer-assisted design (CAD) systems and electronic music generators. We can imagine similar ways in which computer tools enable students to develop new knowledge creatively in many other disciplines. Earlier in this publication, Alice Reich observed that she wanted her young cultural anthropologists to get out into the field; she didn't want them learning about the dissemination of culture by studying computer-based simulations. With this point, I am in complete agreement. So let's add to her ethnographer's backpack a lap-top computer as she sets out for the field. Now as our student ethnographer conducts her interviews, she enters her notes into a very simple word processing program that allows her to search for key words. As the notes accumulate, the student is quickly developing a searchable database of her own, unique information. She is "evolving" a structure that will enable her to turn her rich store of information into new knowledge. Back in her tent or her study, she brings her notes together in many ways—some of which may not have occurred to her otherwise. She tries out these different combinations of material, turns her notes into experimental paragraphs, combines, separates, and stores the notes again for later reference. Beginning with this very simple computer tool, she has been able to create her own body of information and turn it into a useful piece of work.

As computers thus help us make our students into doers rather than listeners—active participants in their own learning—our role as their teachers is bound to change. As Fred Goodman points out so wisely, the teacher becomes something of a "juggler's assistant," supplying the tools, adjusting the flow of information, coaching and monitoring as the students practice their craft and develop their dexterity. But this role, engaging though it may be, cannot define the teacher's role entirely. Old challenges for teaching will remain and new challenges will arise. Sometimes, for instance, students have not developed a firm grasp of basic principles in a discipline. Without a strong foundation, how can they reasonably become active and independent learners? Won't they just practice their errors or reinforce the limitations of their understanding? This is a familiar problem that may be exacerbated in the information-rich learning environment we have envisioned. Where there is such an "instructional bottleneck" (a term coined by Sarosh Talukdar at Carnegie Mellon University to describe concepts that are difficult to grasp but crucial for further learning), faculty members are using well-designed simulations or computer-based exercises to focus students' attention on a particular idea or skill that, once understood or reinforced, will enable a student to proceed to more independent and active learning.

There may be new challenges as well. For instance, we will have to consider the consequences of the success that will come to students who begin to learn by using the tools and the information that computers make available to them. Once Fred Goodman's juniors have constructed their wonderful global simulation and supervised high school students in using it, what should they do as seniors? If this activity has really made them learners in a different way, what are the implications of that learning for their advanced work? What does intermediate Latin look like if first-year students in classics learn their Latin grammar with Daniel Dennett's "hypercube?" Would grammar drills of conjugations not mastered the first time be a thing of the past? Only a few professors are examining the consequences of introducing their students to the use of information technology in a systematic way. One of these is Edward Redish, physics professor at the University of Maryland, who is reconstructing the introductory physics curriculum on the assumption that the computer will enable students to master essential concepts in physics in a logical order not solely dependent on students' progress in mathematics. This reorganization and students' familiarity with computing tools as an integral part of physics education will lead to a rethinking of more advanced courses.

Besides these opportunities for new kinds of learning and new kinds of teaching, students' access to information and to the tools that utilize information poses fascinating opportunities for innovations in the curriculum. In the large research universities, computer tools have "trickled down" into the undergraduate curriculum as faculty members have moved these tools out of their research environments and made them more available to students. But that impetus is much less likely at our small liberal arts college. So let's consider a different strategy. Our curriculum is currently structured around a set of distribution requirements that are meant to provide an introduction to a range of disciplinary methodologies and materials. Only in the natural sciences do we require a laboratory—an organized place and set of exercises for "doing" the work of the discipline. What if we extended that idea of a lab or workshop to all the required courses, to social sciences and humanities, to composition and to foreign language, to mathematics? How much would the curriculum change, and to what benefit for students' learning, if in every distribution course, students had to practice, had to "do it again thoughtfully," had to become an active learner? Many courses already have some such component; others would have to be substantially redesigned. From the examples I have already cited, I think it's clear that information technology would play a significant role in many of those new designs. To offer one speculative example drawn from an earlier presentation here: students learning art history have to know something about making attributions (slide identifications on the midterm exam are, after all, miniature exercises in attribution). Wouldn't it be exciting if students could have access to a laboratory for attribution to a great wealth of images—ears, noses, eyes—on a compact disk that they could examine and compare in order to gain experience the way an expert art historian does, through looking at many examples? Computers could also provide laboratory experience in the use of perspective in Renaissance drawings or in the use of color in modern paintings.

Any substantial infusion into our curriculum of information and of computers that help students gain access to information and manage it, is going to raise a myriad of problems. We can recite the familiar litany. There are too few incentives for faculty to invest time in rethinking their courses to take advantage of new resources.

And even if faculty are willing, the resources at most institutions are scarce; it can be extremely expensive to develop some of the projects I have described. A third problem is particularly worrisome: technology can exacerbate inequities in education both within and across institutions. A fourth problem is often hidden in the excitement that comes with new ideas for improving learning: these experiments are hard to evaluate. We really don't know how to determine whether these new kinds of learning are better, or even exactly how they are different, than traditional methods of instruction.

But these concerns must remain topics for future conversations among us. Despite them, I remain optimistic about the possibility that information technology will *not* drown students in data, but will instead provide the very learning opportunities that our students most need. Let me close by quoting a student at Drexel University. He was a freshman engineer who took a technical writing course in which his professor, Valarie Arms, introduced him to word processing. When asked to evaluate the course he said, with amazement and with pleasure, "The computer is like a window on my own ideas."

That statement is a valuable and important one with which to conclude our conference. It serves to remind us that information technology, in the last analysis, should come into the classroom to provide students with unlimited access not simply to more and more data—but to the wealth of ideas in their own minds.

NOTE

1.   The material in this talk owes much to the work of the FIPSE Technology Study Group (1984-88) and their report, *Ivory Towers, Silicon Basements: Learner-centered Computing in Postsecondary Education* (McKinney, TX: Academic Computing Publications, Inc., 1988).

UNLIMITED INFORMATION ACCESS: "EMPOWERING UP" OUR INSTITUTIONS

LEN CLARK

Deans are almost never asked their opinion about anything. When we offer opinions, usually unsolicited, we are not taken to have offered opinions but to have offered emerging policies. Then if someone in the English department is around, of course, those are negatively reviewed immediately. So it's great to brainstorm some.

One reason I was asked was because of my local fame in futurology on area networks. I am one of those people who in 1982 or thereabouts, on the basis of overwhelming evidence (in addition to a special kind of insight that I have) predicted we ought all to downsize our operations because of the impending decline in the college age population, which would result in smaller colleges. My second prediction was that we had about reached the limit on tuition increases and we were going to have to live within our means. Through all, I fortunately have retained my modesty.

My perspective is that of a person who has responsibilities for helping to formulate overall institutional vision. What happens when a question like the impact of unlimited information comes together with some areas of major responsibilities for me? I'll discuss several needs I see though not in equal detail: to formulate an overall vision of the curriculum, to attend to issues of faculty development, to create self conscious understanding of institutional

---

Clark is Provost and Academic Dean, Earlham College, Richmond, Indiana.

rewards, and to give attention to organization charts and their effects on institutional operations.

First, I take it that deans and other institutional administrators ought to have a pretty firm view of what the overall curriculum in their institution is trying to accomplish. For many of us, it is through the curriculum as well as co-curricular activities, that we aim to enable students to live lives of significance. To do that we find that we must empower them. In fact, all four headings I'm going to talk about have to do with empowering.

We have asked at this forum why do we presume that empowering is so important and that it's always good? That's a legitimate question—I think a good and important one and central to what I do every day. The biggest reason it is so important to me is that it is not a matter of super-charging a functioning vehicle: It is rather a much more sobering assessment that empowering is making whole something that may be broken or unhappily incomplete—more like charging a battery in a car, which isn't going to function unless you and others can help get it moving. Empowering is a very serious problem in this whole society, it seems to me.

But empowering students to live lives of significance is at the heart of what I take our curricular responsibilities to be. One of my pat ways of saying how I think liberal arts education tries to accomplish that is to engage students with the powers and the limits of the disciplines. How do you do it? How do you accomplish introducing to students, and increasing their facility in, the powers and the limits of disciplines?

You don't do it by amassing greater and greater piles of data. We've talked about that. We've tried to conceive how to say that. Martin Dillon talked about encouraging learned incapacity when we focus on gathering of data to the exclusion of the "selects" or filters we put on it. I confess I am one of those who didn't understand at first why Trivial Pursuit was a trivial pursuit, but it is only that. The point of that title is something we should be emphasizing in our attempt to move beyond information gathering and access to unlimited pieces of data as necessarily good. We all know that, but we also have to confess to one another, it must be very deep in our consciousness that collecting things is somehow a good.

We have also discovered through painful experience over the last couple of decades that compulsive over-attention to detail is no remedy. By introducing first term freshman to our view of the structure of the disciplines, we've bored the devil out of them several times.

I suppose the most powerful educational example of what I hope we would institutionally promote in regard to the relating of information and the processing of information occurred in a course some colleagues gave in 1972-73 at Earlham. It was a course on contemporary Japan in which a historian, a political scientist, and a philosopher introduced students to the literature of the Nixon shocks—the period when Nixon made overtures to China without telling Japan that he was going to do so. There was tremendous reaction from the Japanese press, then stunned reaction in the American press and more reaction in the Japanese press, among government officials, all over the place. What this team did was present students with all the information needed to try to figure out what happened and why it happened. These were students who were naive to the culture, by and large, but plenty of information was given. They were given several days to use that information to come up with theories.

What happened was called in an earlier presentation, a systematically produced "information overload," in which students began groping almost randomly for organizational principles. Then these saviors on disciplinary horses came in and disagreed with one another on what the organizational principles ought to be. The political scientist said, "I understand your consternation with all this information. The way to deal with that is to understand that social and political organizations, like states, work on the principle of power. Now let's locate what the power issues are." As a good political scientist, he began laying out the disciplinary structure that would help them to understand those issues. The historian predictably came up and said, "That's not really the issue, you have to understand the historical context in which this occurred," and began to teach them some history. The philosopher tried to point out that unless you understood the religious and ethical background within which political and value questions were considered, you would never understand historically or politically why the Japanese reacted as they did.

I think that was terrific education and the more we can duplicate that kind of challenge to students to present them not just with the informational overload, but then with resources, the greatest of which are our disciplines, the better off we are. We have known at least since Hume that we can think of information as a collection of bits of data that when added together give you a collection of bits of data. Some sense of the representative structure of their reality is necessary. If we think of unlimited information as a collection of bits, then of course we are going to denigrate it. But we don't need to think of information that way.

I think there are several themes about what information in a larger sense could be that make access to unlimited information a really exciting educational challenge. Here is a quick list to review; it collects in some ways what has already been said.

Unlimited access to information can be liberating and empowering when it is access first to varying theories and their critics. Jerry Woolpy's work with the Science Citation Index is a good example of how that can be done. We institutional administrators need to prepare for providing access to those indexes as they become available in field after field. They aren't everything, but they are introductions to argument, not just to information. That's great.

A second really powerful sense of access we can get, if we think of information broadly, is access to patterns of data, so that students can themselves theorize. Fred Wakeman, current head of the Social Science Research Council, was asked to review new research currents in the social sciences at an Association of American Colleges meeting in Washington. He said one of the most exciting was that the power of computing was now making available together, visually, patterns that people might not otherwise have put together. You can relate variables, put them up there and look at them and look for relationships you might never have guessed were there.

He also said relevant to our theme that one of the most exciting aspects of this revolution is that it is accessible even to undergraduates. The making of theory by the suggestive juxtaposition of patterns of different kinds of data is one of the most exciting things that's happening.

A third kind of unlimited information notion is access to voices of others. I've used Jerry Woolpy's Delphi technique in an introductory philosophy class and found it a marvelous way to get information in this broader sense that students don't get any other way. One of the voices we have added access to that way is that of the silent discussant—the person who appears in class to be thinking like crazy, about two steps behind the fastest talkers, but never says anything because the discussion is already gone by the time he or she has thought what to say. But these persons may have the wisest contributions in the whole class to the education of their peers. For students to have access to the silent ones through something like Delphi, where they can sit down and consider the opinions of other students, then type their responses when ready, is access in a new and wonderful way, I think.

We must not forget one's own voice as a fourth kind of information to which students now have access. The notion of word processing as providing access to one's own voice in ways that writing out a text didn't, is an important thing to be celebrated and to be maximized.

Finally, if we think of information in relation to the curriculum in the way Daniel Dennett urged us to, as access to filters and metafilters particularly, I think we will allow students to be more self conscious of the ways they impose disciplinary and other frameworks on data and in turn, of ways they are lead and narrowed by it. Roughly, it's a case of learning the impact of the selects that you run.

My 19-year-old, when he was looking at colleges, decided to do it in the scientific way and use a program that many high schools have for selecting the college that would be just right for him. He came home with a printout. I never did figure out how he did this, but he ended up with Vincennes University, a two-year university in southwestern Indiana; Marietta College, a four-year liberal arts college on the Ohio River; and the Ohio School of Podiatry in Columbus. He is now at a liberal arts college.

There are tremendous impediments to our becoming self conscious about our selects. Somebody mentioned Robert Bellah's *Habits of the Heart*. The most at-home and depressing part of Bellah's analysis is the tremendous reservoir of respect for pluralism our students and we have—respect for pluralism, which forces us to say, "Well, I'm such and such a filterer," but also gives us almost unlimited tolerance for everybody else's filters.

We need to develop in students the discipline, and in institutions the disciplines, to criticize the filters, and I would reinforce that as a real institutional priority. Those are several ways in which I think our highest aspirations for the curriculum can be enhanced (or damaged if we're not careful) by the impact of unlimited information.

In many ways I believe the key problem in faculty development is the issue of empowerment. It is not the issue of motivating faculty to work harder. It is not the need to excite faculty about new areas of inquiry, although to have those opportunities are important.

I think a colleague has put his finger on some of the dimensions of the problem in a piece of research he is doing. His thesis is that western society for the last couple hundred years or so, has looked at ethics, religion and social behavior from a focus of overcoming or dealing with guilt. Our individual and social model is that we live in a world in which most of the important choices we face are ethical dilemmas in which the way to live a bad life is to do the wrong thing and then have to seek forgiveness for it. There also is a very deeply rooted set of themes in Christian and Jewish traditions dealing with shame as the counterpart to guilt. Shame is that feature of our consciousness that reflects our inability to do enough—the feeling that we can't ever be worthy. It is sometimes reflected in the diagnosis of clinical depression, in which the problem is not a sense of having done something wrong, but rather a feeling of disability to do anything worthy. We heap a lot of almost unlimited obligations on ourselves.

Is new technology going to move us toward obsolescence of teachers? Oh no. You are going to have to work harder. There is much more to do and, moreover, it's of tremendous moral significance what you do. You can really screw those kids up now, if you don't work hard enough.

One of the most marked things I have seen since I began teaching in the mid-sixties is an increasing emphasis on evaluation of teaching, thereby turning up the pressure in many of our institutions on the teaching-research dilemma, and further increasing our sense of the importance and moral significance, of teaching. As we worry more whether the liberal arts can survive, we see an increasing significance and need for the liberal arts, and therefore want our teachers to do better at the same time we question the vulnerability of the whole project.

I think access to unlimited information has some two-edged impact on that. One impact is maybe the readiness students will have for information, to get us over the hump of the new teachers who head themselves toward early burnout by packing lectures with incredible amounts of information. Most of you veteran teachers can remember how miserably over-prepared you were the first couple of years. You were so over-prepared that you couldn't listen to students, deviate easily from an outline, or attend to many of the most important educational things we ought to be doing. If the sheer clear presence of information makes that part of what we do more obsolescent, I think it can liberate young teachers to think sooner about what it is their vocation really calls them to do in the classroom. I wish I knew how to help make sure that the good impact of unlimited information in that sense were realized. A group of us at Earlham are talking about somehow finding real ways to help first year teachers enter more slowly into the pace of classroom teaching in what has turned out to be a very fast track in American liberal arts colleges. I would welcome further discussion on how we can lower the pressure and liberate people to affirm themselves and feel empowered as they move into this profession.

First on the organization chart—the way in which we organize the academic enterprise to empower people to take advantage of the good parts of unlimited information access—underlines the need for librarians, computer folks and teaching faculty to be part of the same team. This is something we ought to try very hard to accomplish.

When I came to Earlham, one of the five elected faculty members on the faculty affairs committee—which interviewed all new people and advised the president on all promotion in contract renewal and tenure decisions—was college librarian Evan Farber. I didn't think there was anything unusual about that. I was a new faculty member; I assumed that librarians were central to the teaching enterprise. The more we can move toward that kind of pattern of shared responsibility in and out of the classroom, the better off we will be.

As regards institutional rewards, I know by our personnel policies we sometimes signal what's important in ways that are unintentional and that do great damage in institutions. The acting president of Earlham, before Dick Wood came on board, is a fellow who was on loan to us from business. He said, "always remember you get more of what you *inspect* than of what you *expect*." If you want more of something, count it and let people know you're counting it. So the question of software development and whether that gets rewarded is important.

Adapting to software in the computer revolution or unlimited information access is not really the problem. It is continued confusion about the relationship between research and teaching in the mission of institutions. We would do very well if we tried to clarify (not only for institutions, but for parts of institutions and for individual positions) whether the mission of a college or university is to add to the sum of knowledge, or whether the mission of that college or university is to educate undergraduate students.

If it's teaching, you say research is important but we value it because it liberates us to teach effectively. If you're at a research institution, you say students are going to come here to study with you, not because you're a good teacher particularly but because you are an eminent scholar who can show student apprentices how to do what you do.

If we were clearer about that, we would be self conscious about some of these problems in regard to what we reward and what we don't; we would also help empower by liberating faculty from the crushing load of vacillating administrations, which often come in with a new dean or new president who says, "Thirty percent research and 70 percent teaching is about right—but boy, that 30 percent research is really important, know what I mean?" This kind of leadership is not liberating to anyone.

To sum up, the way we think about information is going to help us avoid some of the ugly downside of that and may help us do our jobs better. How generally can we characterize the way to respond affirmatively to unlimited information access? Probably by focusing on empowering the individual in issue after issue, case after case. We probably cannot do better than that.

EMPOWERMENT AS INFRASTRUCTURE: PLANNING THE CAMPUS

THOMAS J. HOCHSTETTLER

As an academic administrator, I deal on a daily basis with issues of empowerment at a very fundamental level. Let us descend for the moment from the heady realm of ethical and moral dilemmas confronting academicians, dilemmas centering on whether technological innovation by itself in any way adds value to the educational process, or more importantly, adds or ever could add a modicum of wisdom to the sum total of human experience. For me, it is enough to know that, ranked against all the tools that have been used to educate people since time began, the technological advances of the last two or three decades hold at least some relative promise of furthering the human quest for understanding. More to the point, no administrator at this point in history could conceivably survive by ignoring the possibility that computer technology might play a role, indeed a very large role, in the life of a college or university. When I speak of empowerment, therefore, it is empowerment of a very basic kind. It is an empowerment that is afforded the scholar simply through having access to the widest possible range of tools. In short, it is the empowerment that comes from solid, responsive infrastructure.

At Bowdoin College, I am charged not only with line responsibility for computing on campus but also with the task of

---

Hochstettler is Dean for Planning and General Administration and Lecturer in History, Bowdoin College, Brunswick, Maine.

coordinating the planning for the future of the college, both academic and administrative. I am indeed fortunate that a series of historical coincidences has brought these two areas of responsibility together within a single vice-presidential area at Bowdoin. It was pure happenstance that in 1987, Bowdoin decided to hire a chief planning officer at the same juncture that it decided to create a senior officer for information services. It was only natural that those two positions be conjoined. As Bowdoin's first dean for Planning and General Administration, I enjoy a unique perspective from which to make judgments concerning the future configuration of the college and the disposition of its resources. Planning for the technological infrastructure of our institution, therefore, can not avoid the context of planning for the academic program of the college as a whole for the next decade and beyond.

Before proceeding further, let me admit to a concern I have even in broaching the topic of planning for a technological infra-structure before an audience so diverse as this one. How can I, or anyone for that matter, hope to impart useful information—let alone wisdom—to an audience of this type. Represented here are faculty and administrators who are technologically very sophisticated indeed. We have heard, however, that there are others among us who consider an electric typewriter upon their desks something of a technological infringement upon a proper academic workstyle. Moreover, represented here are both large and small institutions, great public institutions and small liberal arts colleges. I know from ten years of working at Stanford University that the quality of the issues and the way they are handled are very different between large and small institutions. So rather than try to address all constituencies, I will limit myself to those issues that pertain primarily to the small liberal arts colleges.

We at Bowdoin are currently in the process of putting together a ten-year plan for the college. We are also thinking seriously about the longer term, about what kind of institution we want to bequeath to those who come after us, say, after the year 2010. Our approach is frankly a pragmatic one, since our planning must be built upon our own very particular history, must meet the needs of our own idiosyncratic faculty, and must take constant heed of the limits imposed by the relative scarcity of space, money and personnel. As we examine the future of computing at Bowdoin, we are perhaps even more influenced by the past than we are in planning for other areas of the college. For one thing, we have the history of our computing staff. Twenty years ago, we hired a director of computing who remains in that position to this day. Whereas another institution might have decided that newer blood would better suit the exigencies of an evolving environment, we, like many other small schools, have gladly retained the services of our long-time staffers simply because they tend to be omnicompetent. Any individual who remains in place within an institution for two decades is usually able, and sometimes willing, to do many more jobs than someone with a similar title at a large institution. The point is that the small scale of operations within the small liberal arts college sometimes makes it difficult to instigate radical changes of any sort without incurring significant, if not overwhelming, costs as a consequence. Planning, therefore, must take place in the context of a living past and must take account of the value of inherited personnel and facilities in a way that would be frankly unacceptable in the more competitive environment, of, say, a large research university.

The remainder of my remarks, then, are a litany of suggestions that administrators and faculty alike within the liberal arts environment might use as general guidelines in the process for an enriched technological environment.

The first suggestion: don't expect to be right; don't expect that every decision you are going to make is going to be optimal, because it will not be. You are going to make mistakes. You are going to choose a microcomputer vendor, you are going to choose a mainframe, you are going to equip a laboratory that will be the wrong thing to do. There is no way to get around that. Obviously, such decisions are taken far removed from the ethical issues of what kinds of things one needs to do in order to make the task of teaching easier for the faculty, what sorts of things one has a moral obligation to do to encourage students to ask the right questions, or to examine their own beliefs and their own set of moral values.

I point to two mistakes that we have made at Bowdoin. They are decisions, which over the course of time, we have learned may not have been exactly the best decisions for us to make.

One occurred last summer, in response to what we thought was a good deal of popular demand. We installed a Macintosh lab on campus. The Macintosh environment is the environment with which most of our students are familiar. They are comfortable with it, it is easy to use, and the faculty seemed to like it as well. We thought: what could be better than to provide twenty or thirty computers, which would be networked together with a printer, in a building that housed the mathematics and computer science department, and make that laboratory available for teaching and also for evening work for students who wanted to do stand-alone word processing?

Having sunk some $80,000 into the machinery, another $20,000 into fiber optic cabling, and having put the whole thing together in a fully remodeled classroom, we did a survey of students this fall to find out what they really wanted. A year ago we had ten to twenty percent of our students buying their own Macintosh computers for use in their dormitories. This year that went up to forty percent and by all indications it will be sixty percent by next year. Like many small schools, Bowdoin has a very advantageous purchasing agreement with Apple, and our students can get a fairly good deal on some very good equipment. So we have now equipped this large laboratory, which some faculty love—especially our more junior faculty. The new facility is a pleasure for the faculty to teach in. They are developing their own software. Their colleagues at other institutions have developed software that we can use in this laboratory. But our overriding purpose in developing the lab was to provide access to computing, and particularly to word processing, for students. Now, after all, the students are saying: "No, we don't want to use that."

I recall someone saying recently that students will not go more than eighteen steps away from their dormitory room in order to find the means for doing word processing. Well, here we've built a building that is halfway across campus, a computing center that is now open virtually twenty-four hours a day, and we are finding out that the students are deserting that kind of facility. Did we make a mistake in choosing to build this kind of a computing lab? I don't think so. It was the best decision at the time. It also leaves us flexibility because we can take those machines and we can move them around. We own the machines and we can do with them whatever we want.

Something else has happened that we didn't expect. It has called forth demand from sections of the college community that we never suspected would be interested in computing. Some faculty members who had no inclination whatsoever in doing anything with microcomputing, especially in the classroom, are now finding that it's extremely useful for things that they had not anticipated.

One other thing that we are in the process of doing is putting in an automated library system. The reason we are doing this is that several of the other colleges in Maine—Colby, Bates, and the University of Maine—are going in together and coordinating our library cataloging and circulation systems. We are going to be making access to each other's collections far easier with this online catalog. It is also going to allow our librarians to catalog things, to keep track of things in the acquisition process in a way that we are at the present time unable to do.

We in Maine have a closed, collegial kind of attitude. One finds this kind of cooperation springing up quite serendipitously in the most unlikely places. Bowdoin has the largest library, the best collection in the state, so that it is not necessarily in our interest to share library resources, because our collection is going to be most at risk. Yet our commitment to the state of Maine, to the people of Maine, and particularly to the poorer people of the state of Maine in trying to bring them into a higher level of education—made this kind of a step a good decision. It is also true that prospective students are apt to think less well of you if you don't have terminals sitting in prominent places throughout your library.

My second guideline is that small schools should try to stay behind the cutting edge of technology. There is absolutely no reason that a school like Bowdoin should be trying to do the sorts of things that a school such as Ohio State University is doing. We simply do not have the resources. We cannot compete, and there is no reason why we should not let the big boys make all the mistakes first and then come along at a slower rate, pick up after they have gone through and worked out all of the bugs.

Right now, for example, we are in the process of evaluating some software that will allow our different operating systems to talk to each other in a far more seamless way than they currently do. At present, in order to get from one of our mainframes to another, one must traverse a very complicated uploading, downloading process. We would like to be able to have a more transparent interface between all those operating systems. The technology has not been there and in my estimation it isn't there yet to allow a school like Bowdoin to have true interoperability. That kind of invisibility is extremely expensive to buy, or at least it has been historically. The cost is going down. You should constantly be watching your cost curve once it comes down far enough that it intersects your utility curve, that is the point when you should buy.

Guideline number three—don't let administration make all of your plans for you. I believe at a school the size of Earlham or Bowdoin there is no reason why the faculty should not be involved in every level of facility planning, of hiring, of looking at the allocation of resources, not only with regard to strictly academic kinds of functions but also in terms of administrative functions. I am sure that at most small institutions, this is the pattern.

I think sometimes faculty do not think of all of the ways in which they could get involved in facility planning. For example, we are in the process at Bowdoin of building a new science center, which is going to force our language and media faculty to relocate. There is a plan on the books to put the media center in the library. The logic behind this plan centered on the notion that the media center serves as a distribution point for video tapes. The college, like all colleges, is building a very substantial library of video tapes, and the librarian and the dean of the faculty believed at the time that those video tapes should be stored somewhere near the front desk of the library, to be checked out and checked back in. The library, then, was the logical place to keep the video tapes. Well, our media center people have far, far more ambitious plans for themselves. They are thinking of a centralized place where they will be doing projection. Several classrooms across campus—one day, maybe all classrooms across campus—will be equipped with projection equipment, and there will be a central place where those films will be projected over fiberoptic networking. The tape will not have to go physically to the site of showing. Thus, valuable library space does not need to be devoted to video storage. The physical location of projection becomes essentially irrelevant. We are beginning now to rethink the possibilities. Now it is unlikely that this kind of technology will be available even in the next two or three years. But we need to begin to position ourselves so that we can take advantage of it when it becomes technically feasible and economically affordable. I think we would be poor stewards indeed if we were to put the video tapes in space that is desperately needed to put books.

I do not really have any simple guidelines for prioritizing the uses of scarce resources. Rule number one would be try not to spend your own money if you can absolutely avoid it. There are plenty of foundations who are anxious and willing to help small colleges with their efforts to develop software for courses. Digital

Equipment Corporation has recently liberalized its policy in terms of discounts it is giving to small colleges. Heretofore Digital gave generous discounts only to very big colleges and universities and colleges with large science faculties. Those rules are beginning to change, not only at Digital but at other large firms. Foundations are also open to the creative kinds of things that many faculty are doing all across the country. The corollary to that rule is that if you have to spend your own money, spend it on proven technology. Avoid buying something that has not proven itself to be effective.

I have another guideline that is a far more difficult thing to follow. Avoid making computing money compete with other kinds of money. When I arrived at Bowdoin, one of the first things that I did was to establish for myself a fund to allow for connectivity between faculty offices and the mainframe. This move was made with an eye toward one day allowing faculty to communicate via electronic mail, not necessarily with other people on campus but with colleagues across the country or across the world. It makes a lot of sense, and sooner or later it will be nice to have that capability.

One of the first things we discovered, however, was that providing the wire and the terminal was really almost rapidly becoming too little for faculty members. What they really wanted was a microcomputer attached to that line, and the marginal cost for doing that, it turned out, was only about $1,000 or so. So we decided that we would provide a microcomputer to those faculty members who wanted it and put those requests through a faculty committee. That worked fairly well for about a year. It only worked because the dean of the faculty was on sabbatical and he didn't realize that I was in the process of providing faculty with microcomputers. When he came back, in his very kind way, he asked me if he couldn't please have at least the microcomputer fund back. I relinquished it and in the course of events the money was cut out of his budget. My point is that computing deserves to be treated as a serious, permanent part of the academic endeavor in the same way that the library is a serious, permanent part of the academic endeavor. Institutions need to begin, in whatever fashion and to whatever extent, to fund the ongoing presence of computing in academia. When our computing director first arrived he established a pattern of capital funding for major computing purchases for the college in six figures on an annual basis. That amount has served us extremely well for a college of only 1,350 students and a faculty of about 130 to 140. That's a very good computing budget at the present time, although it pales in comparison to the money that is spent by a school like OSU or Stanford or The University of Michigan. But unless a school is prepared to spend those kinds of resources on an annual basis, that school is going to have trouble. One day the technological revolution will break upon that institution, and it will have to play some very serious catchup.

There they are, a string of gratuitous guidelines for planning for computing in the liberal arts college approaching the threshold of the twenty-first century. As I said at the outset, it is somewhat presumptuous to assume that remarks of this kind can have general applicability for an audience as diverse as this one. In conclusion, I make one more gratuitous comment, but one that I hope does have general applicability. Whatever you do, do not ignore computing, hoping against hope that it will go away. I am perplexed to hear that old mentors and colleagues are so averse to trying out the new technology, even in the most obviously useful ways. I am perplexed likewise that educators feel such apprehension at the flood of information that the technological revolution has swept upon us. There can be, from my perspective, no turning our backs on the new accessibility of information. For better or worse, we can not responsibly refuse to acknowledge the changes that are forcing their way into the classroom.

MAKING IT ALL HAPPEN

WARREN BRYAN MARTIN

Three assumptions seem to me to run through the theme of this forum on "Teaching and Technology." All of them have both a positive and a cautionary tone.

The first assumption is that changes in degree have a way of becoming changes in kind. The novelist John Barth makes this point dramatically: "The day grows darker and darker and then it is night. Water grows colder and colder and then it is ice. A man grows older and older and then he is dead. Changes in degree become changes in kind."

When science and technology produced the atom bomb and later the hydrogen bomb, we moved not just from one form of weaponry to another, as when gunpowder superseded bows and arrows and spears. We moved from the confrontation of rival armies in the field to the threat of nuclear weapons affecting whole populations, and beyond to the possibility through nuclear war of ending civilization as we've known it. The level of peril has been heightened to the extent that, regarding warfare, changes in degree have greatly increased the prospect of changes in kind.

Surely it's safe to say that certain technologies of this technological society have achieved an importance all out of proportion to their cost or size, and, that this is the case with computer technology and telecommunications. We are not dealing with changes equivalent to the change from an ice box to a

---

Martin is Senior Fellow, at the Carnegie Foundation for the Advancement of Teaching.

refrigerator. We are talking about tools and techniques with such marvelous speed, capacity, and resourcefulness that they're significantly changing society and may indeed be leading to its transformation—radically amplifying the work of our minds. These machines store and retrieve and process and refine information at speeds beyond all prior experience and established expectations, and even as all of this is happening we see the emergence, dare we say it, of reasoning machines. These are changes in degree showing potential, at least, for effecting changes in kind.

The second assumption relates to the first, but extends its meaning and adds a warning. When changes in degree become changes in kind, one of the consequences is that persons who have no direct contact with those changes and certainly no control over them are nevertheless directly affected. Indeed, these persons may be affected to such an extent that their lives will never be the same again. Great masses of people found their lives directly and radically changed by the industrial revolution without ever operating a steam engine or a cotton picking machine, an invention that took away the work of masses of southern black farm laborers and helped turn them from farms to cities, resulting in changes in the demographics of America that led, among other things, to the civil rights movement.

Now, for better or worse, schools, colleges, and universities are purchasing computer equipment that promises more than is being delivered. It's also evident that some of the effects that have been delivered are more negative than positive. The computer called "user-friendly" has not always been friendly to users, and, in fact, is often downright unfriendly to non-users. Two authors, Clapp and Rosak, warn not only about overload, boredom, and what has been called the "dazzle effect" of technology, they also point out the extent to which the computer makes possible the exclusionary use of information as well as the status it confers, exacerbating class differences and encouraging "the cult of information."

Technology now will accomplish with the aid of one-third of the work force that for which two-thirds of the work force is no longer needed. Nearly everybody's life is thereby influenced. The numerical majority, the poor and the working class, will have to accommodate because of this elite revolution to the culture favored by the technologically sophisticated minority—the wealthy, the affluent, the middle class. This is the equity issue that has surfaced occasionally in these articles and about which there are differences of opinion.

The third assumption adds to the point that changes in degree become changes in kind, affecting persons not directly involved as much or more as those directing the changes. I now add the idea, also widely shared, that means are ends in the process of evolving.

Society suffers from a growing gap between peaks of factual information and the slower processes of teasing out meanings—especially shared values—worked out usually in the valley of human experience rather than at the peaks. When the meanings do not come forward in stride with the means then the techniques of technology take on a life of their own, and make their own meaning. That kind of power—in a variation of the aphorism attributed to Lord Acton—corrupts and if unchallenged will finally corrupt absolutely. Our job, especially in liberal arts colleges and in universities with strong undergraduate liberal arts units, is to see that the connections are maintained. But most of us here have a sense that there are dangers in technology's power that, if we do not watch out, will tempt us to make the developed countries too much into a computer.

We're told that this world has a fragile ecology and that we must protect our environment and effect change slowly. Whether we agree on that or not, I am among those persons who are persuaded that we have in the western nations now a very fragile culture held together by an increasingly strained social consensus. Changes of the magnitude we are discussing frighten me, not because I'm especially wise, nor because I'm especially old (although the last is true), but because evidence mounts that the promise of the new technology is equalled by its perils. Shakespeare expresses my sense of anxiety: "The bay trees in our country are all withered and meteors fright the fixed stars of heaven. The pale faced moon looks bloody on the earth and lean-looked prophets whisper fearful change."

At this time, then, when computer science and computer technology are generating changes that seem destined to transform, not merely reform, American culture; at a time when these changes profoundly affect people who are not effecting the changes; at a time when means and ends, technical competency and human understanding seem so hard to keep together, surely we agree that colleges have an awesome special responsibility.

With that statement, I turn from the aforementioned assumptions to several assertions—certain of which are widely shared while a few others may be arbitrarily imposed. I assert that the liberal arts college, and the college of arts and sciences of a strong university are the best institutions in society to put computer technology in proper perspective—I mean, specifically, historical and social perspective and moral perspective.

One way to go about the first task, that of putting technology into historical and social perspective, would be to use the resources of general and liberal education to help students understand that while there's room for differences of emphasis in the conflict and connection between the old and the new, between the specialist and the lay person, they as society's future leaders must never surrender the connections. Tradition and innovation, the expert and the lay person, must go everywhere together.

That's a hard lesson for Americans, especially for young students, but it is as important as it is difficult, even in this "new" country, which is only a little over 200 years old. As Renford Bambrough of Cambridge University has put it, "The problems are always set by an inherited understanding, and the resolution of problems inherited from traditional understanding must also be sought, at least in part, by attention to the inherited understanding." That's true when thinking not only of politics and social thought, or education as a specialized field, but about the whole range of human knowledge—physics, mathematics, science, and technology included. The institution of higher education therefore examines tradition in the presence of this new culture that features change, innovation, and experimentation. The appeal of reason must always be to what is already there in our common stock. The background, the framework for any question, is a set of settled answers to other questions. It's impossible, incoherent, to try to make all things new.

Critics of this position aim their big guns when they say, "Well, what you offer may be acceptable for dealing with the great questions about good and evil, about the direction of human life, but is there not a risk that this line of thought will block the way to development and discovery in science and technology and also in arts and sciences? Or are you saying that everything is adequate or even perfect, that nothing can be changed?" Of course, I'm not arguing there's no need for change. Rather, I'm trying to say something about the way in which those who wish to make changes must conduct their inquiries if they are to be credible in defending the changes they propose. Frances Bacon, in one of his essays, said, "There can be an occasion when reformation is required," but he, even in his century, while recognizing the need for change, went on to say, "It must be the need for reformation that requires the change, not a restless desire for change pretending a reformation." Today, as in the past, the experts have their specialized knowledge and experience that they bring to bear on the questions that trouble us all. And we must listen to them and read them and ponder well their well-informed thoughts and their researched plans. But we remember and we must not allow them to forget that they are at last answerable, especially in the American system of government, to the lay understanding of the general citizenry, just as the individual teacher, also an expert, must speak to his or her pupils' lay understanding.

The expert in any field—Einstein or a college teacher—must make contact with the received understanding of the non-expert, and overturning it can be achieved properly only by showing the profoundest understanding of what we have inherited. The understanding of the past, at its best, requires the reform and motivates the proposed revolution. Telecommunications and the computer, both of which feed on the new, must be reminded of roots that go deep into an old tradition that nourishes the new and even tolerates novelty. Also, those persons who are experts on this transformation must be helped to remember the extraordinary importance for them of the ordinary understanding of these things.

Another way to bring the emerging so-called computer culture into better perspective—this time the moral perspective—is to assert, despite controversy, that while we may say there are no limits to learning, we do anguish over the probability that there are limits to our uses of learning.

Where to draw the line? One place I would draw the line is at having technology substituted in counseling for a therapist, or having computers installed, as is being done, as mechanical psychotherapists—not on the ground that the project is technically infeasible, but on the ground that it's just plain immoral. Much of what we call knowledge we owe to science and technology, but as important as they are, they can also become addictive drugs. And as happens with so many drugs under increasing dosage, science can be converted into a slow-acting poison. Therefore, an important warning should be among the services provided by colleges and universities, a warning about the necessity for contextual thinking to make connections to keep things in moral perspective.

There is more to be said. In our colleges the concern over computer integration into the curriculum should be less of an economic and more of a conceptual issue. Our strategy for thinking through the roles of computers falls back on thinking through the entire curriculum—in its component parts, yes, but also as a statement of collegiate mission.

Apple Computer Company's weekly publication, *Apple Viewpoints*, invited certain of the company's theoreticians back in September 1988 to predict some developments in the next five to ten years. Allen Kay said,

> When we think about how humans have extended themselves over several hundred thousand years of our existence, two main pathways become obvious. The first is through amplifying tools, physical tools, such as the lever, wheel, and steam engine, and figurative tools, such as language, mathematics and computer programs.

The first "M" word, says Kay, is manipulation.

> The second main pathway for human extension is goal cloning—convincing others to work together on our goals. When a group of humans unites to work on some aim, whether it's a small one like the formation of a scout troop or as large as forming a major company, a special kind of machine has to be put together.

The "M" word for this expansion, he says, is management.

Not surprisingly the construction of intelligent processes that can be managed has proven to be much more difficult than designing an amplifying tool. Now, it is at this point where Kay leaves the question of the ability of the computer to move from the muscular and iconic to the abstract world of the symbol, which his colleague at Apple, Stewart Green, picks up:

In computing, the movement is from institutional operation with an operator; to personal, user-friendly; to impersonal community-oriented past, present, future. Also from data, numbers, to information aimed at answering questions, to, in the future, knowledge reflecting experience and, hopefully, wisdom too, drawing on the shared epistemology of a community. The technology has shifted from the calculation of numbers and regular data relations to the presentation of related words and pictures. The shift to a knowledge-based culture will require tools which support the dynamism of connection, association, embracing the user's total experience. The computer will be absorbed in the environment, losing its separate identity. At the introduction of any shiny new technology the holders of the machinery are in the driver's seat, but with maturity the technology becomes a commodity and economic success shifts to those who add value and support infrastructure—in short, to those who add perspective.

Maybe we teachers fear technology so much because we have met the enemy and the enemy is us. Most teachers do what the computer has done—transfer data, information, technique. We've erred on the side of the collection and packaging of disparate data and information, encouraging technical competence narrowly defined and, with it, our specialties and sub-specialties. As computers shift toward connections, toward the interpersonal, toward community, so the curriculum and faculty must make audacious moves in the same direction. If we insist on holding the old ground of separation and specificity, we're going to be ground under by the computer. It will beat us down. If we stay back, the computer networks are going to move on to occupy the very ground that we should quite properly be holding and have as our strength. On the other hand, if we see that our job is to mix ideas and information, to bring creativity and criticism to otherwise inert data, to remind students that the data were made for man (I speak generically), not man for the data, if we bring perspective to information and transform it into knowledge seasoned with a trace of wisdom, then we need not fear the tool—the machine.

Here is another related assertion. To do the job that is rightfully ours and needs to be done, we're going to need to reconceptualize as well as revitalize the undergraduate teacher. Today, in the best-known liberal arts colleges, there is great excitement about the emergence of the so-called research college, where faculty draw students into research projects shared at the undergraduate level, hoping of course to tap into NSF and other lucrative sources of funding. But let us ask, especially in these liberal arts colleges where this research orientation is joined with the subject-matter specializations and majors, whether there are faculty members equally committed, equally skilled, equally well informed about general education? Is the college equally proud of faculty and students who have learned to sort out complex options, unravel a skein of thought, and then finally make good choices and, thus, show a capacity for sound judgment?

The faculty we need more than narrow specialists and technicians are those faculty members who have a specialization but are committed to cross-fertilization, committed to developing interpersonal and community-oriented themes about which those leaders at Apple were talking when projecting the future of the computer. We need more faculty who will acquaint themselves with the literature on student development, and who have perspective on the main features of one or two cognate disciplines adjacent to their own fields (to do so would help re-emphasize the divisional structure of the undergraduate experience). The faculty I'm trying to describe would also have acquaintance with prevailing method-ological orthodoxies, at least in their cognate disci-plines—structuralism and deconstruction and post-modernism, analytic philosophy and phenomenological existentialism, plus others. The aim would be to help the student understand how particular subject matter relates to the student's other academic experiences.

Clapp says, "In twenty-five years of teaching, while I have encountered countless faculty members who consciously sought to bring the best of their own specialization to the students in their classes, I could not find any of my colleagues who were concerned to think about how that subject matter relates to the student's other educational experiences." The task, then, would be to encourage a student's capacity for sound judgment by having a faculty committed to that task as much as we have faculty committed to making an institution into a research college.

Evan Farber said that it's very hard to effect change. But American higher education has been changing for well over 100 years. There have been changes within land grant universities, research universities, community colleges, plus other changes, such as the capture of American higher education by the federal government—first mobilization in the first World War, nationalization in the second World War, and, currently, near coaptation with 30 to 60 percent of the research funding coming from federal sources, often defense-related sources. Clearly we have been changing. And we now propose research colleges to serve as a countervailing force to earlier changes like the development of comprehensive colleges and universities. We will change. The question is whether are we going to try to be in charge of it.

An epic reveals itself most lucidly in its art forms; and from the arts we get sight and insight into what people believe about human nature and their experiences, the things most cherished and most feared. Through art we can look back and look forward, and now we can look around the corner to the new century.

I want, in conclusion, to turn to the arts for guidance as we think about the future. Robertson Davies, the great 75-year-old Canadian novelist, poet, playwright and master of Massey College at the University of Toronto, was recently asked if there was a central theme running through his novels. He replied, "Yes, but I hesitate to mention it because it's so ordinary." "However," he went on, "here it is: the movement of a person, a spirit, from innocence to experience." What this artist takes as his theme, we could take for higher education. Our goal should be to help each student know the movement of a person, of a spirit, from innocence to experience—not to the end that the person is unable to believe because of experience, but rather in order for his or her experience to become informed not only by personal developments but also by the experiences of nature and the world and all that makes us cherish it.

Isomi Naguchi, the great Japanese sculptor of the wonderful rounded stones in the magnificent magical gardens, was a person with an Asian aesthetic who lived between two worlds. He was a person obviously unapologetically rooted in tradition, who always brought forward what he thought was the best of the ancient varieties. And yet those old values, in his hands, always seemed to point in an exemplary fashion to the new, bringing together somehow the old and the new. Naguchi's aesthetic values and accomplishments should be our goal.

We, in liberal arts colleges and comprehensive universities, should be deeply rooted in tradition, unapologetically so, speaking often for enduring truths, whether in biology or other disciplines. And yet in our hands if we're skilled enough and committed enough, those truths can point in exemplary fashion toward the new, perhaps even reconciling old and new. The orientation of Naguchi and Davies, I think, point to a successful reconciliation of teaching and technology.

Universities and colleges with as much interest in a vital campus culture as in efficient management systems, where leadership balances technical competence with human sensitivity, where there is an encouragement for innovation but within the tradition of and with almost an obsession for the inter-connectedness of things, where there's an acknowledgement of symbiosis but also where moral seriousness marks meaning or ways of life—these places are the ones most likely to combine adaptation and distinctiveness. Such institutions not only stand out in the spectrum of colleges and universities that taken together make up the so-called system of higher education in America, but, as coherent communities they also stand as prototypes for an America where the social cement is crumbling, and a new and better way of holding the nation together must be found. The challenge goes that far, that high, that deep.

APPENDIX A

FORUM PARTICIPANTS

Laurence Alvarez	University of the South
Joanne Badagliacco	Pomona College
Vern Bailey	Carleton College
Jerry Bakker	Earlham College
Marilyn Baldwin	Dana Foundation
Diane Balestri	Princeton University
Ruth Barton	The Colorado College
Michael Bell	Grinnell College
Janice Biros	Drexel University
Sarah Blanslei	Lafayette College
Malcolm Blowers	University of North Carolina/ Asheville
Sandra Bolster	Berea College
Raymond Brebach	Drexel University
Rowland Brown	OCLC, Online Computer Library Center, Inc.
John Byrnes	Wabash College
Anne Caputo	Dialog
Lloyd Chapin	Eckerd College
Bill Child	Carleton College
Len Clark	Earlham College
Marshall Cromyn	Reed College
Jan Czechowski	Grinnell College
Marni de laCruz	The Colorado College
Ann de Klerk	Bucknell University
Daniel Dennett	Tufts University
Martin Dillon	OCLC, Online Computer Library Center, Inc.
Paul Dobosh	Mount Holyoke College
Roy Elveton	Carleton College
Evan Farber	Earlham College
David Finley	The Colorado College
Larry Frye	Wabash College
Fred Goodman	The University of Michigan
Carol Grener	Muhlenberg College
John E.H. Hancock	Reed College

Tom Hochstettler	Bowdoin College
Charles Huff	St. Olaf College
Tom Kirk	Berea College
Paul Lacey	Earlham College
Gerald Levin	Bucknell University
Margaret Lichterfeld	Colby College
Ralph Lundgren	The Lilly Endowment
Barbara MacAdam	The University of Michigan
Deanna Marcum	Council on Library Resources
Parker G. Marden	Beloit College
Warren Martin	Carnegie Foundation for the Advancement of Teaching
Joan Marx	Muhlenberg College
Mary Georgia Matlock	Alverno College
Jesse McCartney	Catawba College
William McEachern	Alverno College
Wilbert McKeachie	The University of Michigan
James McKenna	Pomona College
Paul McKinney	Wabash College
Tom Moberg	Kenyon College/Moline
Jon Moline	St. Olaf College
Arnold Ostebee	St. Olaf College
Sara Penhale	Earlham College
Bill Quillian	Mount Holyoke College
Wayne Redenbarger	Ohio State University
Alice Reich	Regis College
James Roth	Alverno College
Richard Sears	Berea College
June Schlueter	Lafayette College
Jacqueline Sheppard	Spelman College
Donald Shive	Muhlenberg College
Allan Smith	Drexel University
J. Brock Spencer	Beloit College
William Stevens	Guilford College
Susan Stine	The Pew Charitable Trusts
Mary Sturgeon	University of North Carolina at Chapel Hill
Carol Stoneburner	Guilford College
Peter Suber	Earlham College
Pat Swanson	The University of Chicago
Sylvia Trelles	Guilford College

Gordon Thompson	Earlham College
Katharine Watson	Eckerd College
Dick Werking	Trinity University
John Wernegreen	Eastern Kentucky University
Kealoha Widdows	Wabash College
Kate Wininger	Earlham College
Jerry Woolpy	Earlham College

APPENDIX B

FORUM ISSUES

TEACHING

1. What will the role of the teacher be?
2. Will the availability of information change teaching from a concept of imparting knowledge to helping students evaluate information?
3. How do you teach standards of judgment and evaluation when students have access to all information?
4. Will the teacher's role be reduced to organizing information?
5. How is total access to information going to affect different disciplines?
6. What will be the impact on teaching when students have access to information unknown to the teacher?
7. As a teacher of X discipline, if you had this assumed technology, how would you use it?
8. How much will faculty learn from students?
9. How will teachers keep up to date?
10. Will technology drive teaching? How can we keep teaching driving technology?
11. To what degree will teaching change from current teacher/student relationship to collaborative relationship?
12. What things now are crucial in an optimum teacher/student relationship that must not be lost?

EDUCATION

1. Will students treat information as knowledge? How best to convey the distinction?
2. What changes from current practices will that mean?
3. How should teachers be prepared to teach in this context?
4. What will be the impact on testing?
5. How can we control plagiarism?
6. How will information technology affect humanities? Differently than the social sciences? Than the sciences?

7.   What is the opportunity to use information technology to raise the quality of teaching and learning?

RESEARCH

1.   How will this technology help a scholar be more productive?

LEARNING

1.   Are there limits to the amount of information with which a human mind can cope? If so, how do we not overstep these limits in the classroom?
2.   What more do we need to know about cognitive development?

MATERIALS

1.   What will textbooks look like? Will we be able to create our own, online texts?
2.   How will we answer the questions of royalties and copyrights?
3.   How do we make materials available most efficiently?
4.   Who should publish, edit, and package materials?
5.   Will we have access just to raw information or will technology organize information to help the students understand it?
6.   How can we evaluate databases when there will be so many, appearing and disappearing frequently?
7.   Who will serve as editors of databases?

CAMPUS INFRASTRUCTURE

1.   What about policies using communication networks on campus and between campuses?
2.   How do we organize to affect change in decentralized education systems?
3.   What are the institutional values and how do they apply to decision making about financial resources for technology?